COMM,

LOST TREASURES
YOU CAN FIND IN
IOWA

Commander's Lost Treasures YOU CAN FIND in the State of Iowa

Commander - J. Hutton Pulitzer, CC, CSA, CSI, ACE

Cover Design and Book Layout by Christopher Cline

Copyright © 2013 NTS, CSI, CSA - National Treasure Society, Cacheology Society and Institute of America, United Kingdom and Cacheology Society of America

TABLE OF CONTENTS

COMMANDER'S
LOST TREASURES

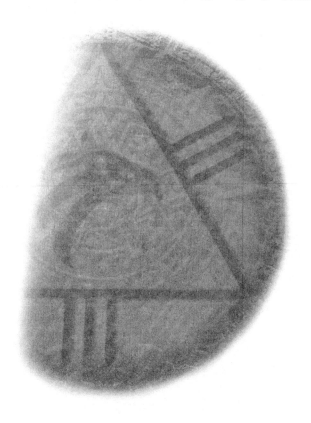

CHAPTER 1

Millions, Billions, or Trillions?

CHAPTER 1 Millions, Billions, or Trillions?

Billions of dollars in lost treasure waiting to be found? That figure must seem outrageous, or at the very least incorrect? If you wondered this to yourself, then you are actually right. There are not billions of dollars out there in lost treasures waiting to be reclaimed. There are trillions of dollars of treasure waiting to be reclaimed. But, I was faced with making a choice when it came to publishing this book. Would I be able to convince the public at large there were millions or even billions to recover, much less trillions? I chose the middle road, a number far more conservative than any realistic assessment. Why?

Most people, right off the top of their heads, could **NOT** tell you how many zeros are in one trillion.

Well, one trillion is 1,000,000,000,000. **1 2 3 4 5 6 7 8 9 10 11 12** - that's **twelve** zeroes.

In fact, to give you a better perspective, in the state of Texas alone, where I am sitting as I write this, there is an estimated $99,581,605,263 (ninety-nine billion) in documented unrecovered lost treasures. Compare that to Florida at $201,608,423,684 (two hundred and one billion) or New Mexico at $365,684,242,105 (three hundred and sixty-five billion) and you can easily see how the numbers rack up. But this is still not quite correct.

The numbers for this book were figured using the daily average price of gold on a day over four months ago. Now, as of this writing, gold is up an additional 32%; this means that Texas treasure is worth $31,866,113,684.16 (thirty-one billion) more, while Florida's treasure is worth an extra $64,514,695,578.88 (sixty-four billion) and New Mexico's an extra $117,018,957,473.60 (one hundred seventeen billion).

Absolutely boggles the mind, does it not? You will learn more about these numbers and where they come from in this book. But first and foremost, this book is not about the values of lost treasures now or in the past, but rather the passion and lore that goes into treasure hunting. If you understand history and treasure and the nature of both, you are moving along the road toward becoming a real treasure hunter. Men have sought out the lost, hidden, stored, and cached treasures of others from the beginning of time. Treasure hunting is thousands of years older than the profession of archaeology, and in fact it is the pursuit of treasure that birthed the profession of archaeology.

There are many forms of treasure seekers, from those who seek documents to those who seek artifacts and mineral sources, since treasure itself comes in many forms. In fact, there are papers and books that have been lost to time which are now as valuable as a ton of gold! There are many different levels of seekers as well. There are the treasure seekers who do it for recreation, those who do it for adventure, and those who do it to shore up historical research. The rarest of the treasure seekers are those who make up the professional class of treasure hunters: those who shun the name treasure hunter, due to the modern implications of that label, and who have gone to the trouble of both the education and certification to become what is professionally called **Cacheologists**.

Cacheology:

> The profession whereby highly trained and certified individuals, using archaeological methods combined with forensic historical research and modern technology, set out to prove or disprove, dispel or recover, set the historical record straight or professionally document, the various types of caches, common treasures or otherwise, that have been lost to history and mankind. The mission of the Cacheologists is to use profit-driven methods to recover lost caches for the expansion of mankind's study, education, instruction, collection, showcasing, and preservation. Cacheology is the professional rescue and preservation of caches that time and the environment would otherwise rapidly and thoroughly destroy, erasing historical records and artifacts vital and irreplaceable for the entire world.

CHAPTER 2

Cacheology

Any Treasure is in fact a cache. A cache is some form of valuables that has been stored, either willingly or under duress, but which was never retrieved. There various forms of caches as well. They are as follows:

1. **C**ache of *Ceremony*

2. **C**ache of *Convenience*

3. **C**ache of *Catastrophe*

4. **C**ache of *Duress*

5. **C**ache of *Criminal Activity*

6. **C**ache of *Nature*

If you understand the nature of a cache, or in other words, if you understand how the cache originally became a cache, you then have a better chance of verifying, locating, and recovering the cache. Below I will give you the formal Cacheological definition of each of these different types of caches, but as you read this book, bear in mind that if you can learn to identify the type of a particular cache, you may have what it takes to become a professional treasure hunter.

CACHE OF *CEREMONY*

A Cache of Ceremony is the style of cache that has been deposited where it was found (or is yet to be found) due to the nature of the culture and ceremonies that generated the cache to begin with. For example, the treasure of King Tut is exactly this type of cache. Ancient Egyptians buried their dead kings with all of their treasures. Their culture, ceremonies, and religious protocols demanded such; thus, the treasure of King Tut is a Cache of Ceremony. So the rule of thumb for a cache identified as a Cache of Ceremony is: If it was the cultural norm for priests, rulers, and/or notables to be buried in a specific religious or ceremonial style and location,. then when you find those you will find the cache. Understand and re-create the ceremony and you can locate the cache.

CACHE OF *CONVENIENCE*

Convenience is exactly that, where it was convenient to store the cache. These caches were not moved from place to place; they were just stored for convenience. It is also the type of cache utilized by workers, common men, and lay people. Why? There are no ceremonies or cultural standards involved in dictating where to stash the cache. For example, it is said there was more money cached away during the Great Depression than there was stored in banks, and billions and billions of that is still cached in the same hiding places. During the Great Depression, people did not trust banks, so they stored their money, valuables and gold in places only known to them, but surely convenient to them. Those places would be in fencepost holes, water wells, fireplaces, floorboards, and such. Another Cache of Convenience, which actually goes hand in hand with a Cache of Catastrophe (defined below), is anywhere a large battle took place. How? Think of the thousands and thousands of soldiers and warriors in time past that would go to war. Along with them they carried their pay (they could not transfer funds to banks back and forth like we did) and their rings, body ornaments, metals, and religious statuaries. Most of these were various forms of precious metals. Before battle, but near the troops actual staging area or camp, each soldier would conveniently (there is that word again) bury his or her personal belongings and fortunes before going into battle. This way they were assured not to lose them and their personal caches would not fall into the hands of the enemy.

Now consider just how many of the warriors would not come back from the battle. Of course, these caches were put there by the attacking army, not any city which was attacked by surprise. So, especially due to invading Roman armies, there are hundreds of thousands, if not millions, of personal soldier or warrior caches in and around camps, staging areas and battlegrounds. 10,000 dead warriors add up to tons of recovered cache troves in each battle area.

CACHE OF *CATASTROPHE*

Catastrophe is a harsh word. A harsh word for harsh circumstances. Disaster, war, earthquake, shipwreck: chose any word that means that people and their places and/or modes of transport are destroyed, then you understand the concept of Cache of Catastrophe.

Spanish and Chinese treasure ships going down in hurricanes are Caches of Catastrophe. Where the catastrophe happened is where the cache was deposited. An ancient temple or library destroyed by a massive earthquake and dropped off into the sea to never be seen again is a Cache of Catastrophe, and where the catastrophe happened, the cache lays in wait for the Cacheologist.

Understand the nature and scope of the catastrophe and you can locate the cache, but remember, by its very nature a Cache of Catastrophe is either at the bottom of the ocean or buried under tons and tons of ancient debris covered in turn by the debris and buildup of time. These caches may be fairly easy to locate but very hard and expensive to recover.

CACHE OF *DURESS*

Logically you might question, "What is really the difference between duress and catastrophe?" The simple answer is **SURVIVAL.** Yes, an unexpected attack of an army or Indians is a catastrophe, and those things and people caught up in the catastrophe ultimately lay exactly where the catastrophe happened. But what about the survivors? There are almost always survivors; how else would we know the historical facts, places, people, and issues, except from those that survived. Indian attacks, routed armies, and flight from pursuers are all causes of caches of duress.

Now put yourself in the survivors' situation. All hell is breaking loose. You grab your family and valuables and haul ass. Literally. The survivor is running away from the catastrophe and invariably the transport of their valuables become too much and they hurriedly bury or conceal their cache to be retrieved later. The outlaws with the posse on their tail does not get the gold or bankroll back to their lair or hideout, they have pursuers right behind them, and they hurriedly bury or stash the cache. They don't have the time or luxury to hide the cache very deep or with

12

much sophistication, or to make sure it's not detectable if someone were to come across it.

So, due to the fact that Caches of Duress are survivors or those on the run from imminent danger, the caches they hide are done hurriedly and on the run, and therefore are not deep or very well hidden. These may be the easiest caches to recover, but due to the nature of the situation, they can be spread over a very large area and may in fact be smaller, though not necessarily less valuable. Find the paths taken by those fleeing and along the way you may find many a cache.

CACHE OF *CRIMINAL ACTIVITY*

Criminals have patterns, partners, and hide outs. Understand those and you understand where to find Caches of Criminal Activity. Yes, in Caches of Duress, I spoke of bandits on the run, so were they not criminals as well, and shouldn't they be listed here? Yes and no. The key is full understanding of the nature of the cache. Yes, the bandit was a criminal, but in that instance, thus the nature of the cache you are seeking, the criminal was on the run being pursued. Therefore they did not reach their hideout, partners in crime, or territory, and they were forced to act under duress.

Remember, understand the nature of the cache and you can find where it is. If you are searching for a trove of gold stolen by Jesse James, and you know that he stole it, fled, and was apprehended (only to escape later), but no gold was found with him, the facts tell you — no, scream to you — that it was stashed on the run. So, do not waste your time looking at his family home or favorite hideout for that particular treasure. But look into the gangsters, bandits, criminals, and drug lords who got away with their ill-gotten goods, and chances are the cache is hidden within their associated network of lairs, hideouts, properties, and partners' properties.

Criminals are notorious for protecting their hidden hoards, and in order to do so the criminal must be within eyeshot, hearing, or quick response distance from the cache. Thus, know the nature of the cache and you can find the cache.

Cache of *Nature*

Gold, platinum, diamonds, sapphires, and such, do not necessarily have to be mined, minted, and shaped into a royal crown to be considered treasure. Nature is the single largest hider and hoarder of caches. Mother Nature is the single richest individual in the world. Bill Gates and Warren Buffet don't even come a close second to her. Mother Nature is so loaded with treasure she can afford to deposit a trillion dollars in gold or diamonds in a single location and never go back to retrieve them, much less expose them, for millions of years. Most treasure hunters forget this source of wealth, but the professional, the Cacheologist is trained to find these caches as well. In fact, to the Cacheologists, this form of cache is considered low-hanging fruit and ends up being the source of funding for their formal cache expeditions.

Millions upon millions of Caches of Nature exist and someone, somewhere in history has stumbled across them and left us a record and facts to follow. The only thing that happened is the original discoverer of the cache could not remember or relocate the exact location of the cache and therefore could never retrieve it. The easiest example of this is the tons of legends and historical facts surrounding lost gold mines. At some point in time, a prospector came across one of Mother Nature's cache hiding places, but by not paying close attention to their surrounding landmarks or through other circumstances, the prospector went into the nearest town to file their claim, get help, or get supplies and tools and could not find their way back to the natural cache site. There is no way to really put a value on these types of caches because one single cache of nature could be worth a trillion dollars in today's precious metals market, and there are literally thousands upon thousands of these found but lost again Caches of Nature.

But following the clues Mother Nature leaves and stories in the historical record of finds, one could find billions in a single location. If you don't believe me, just ask our Canadian friend and diamond expert, Mr. Fripke. Understand the nature of the cache and you can find the cache.

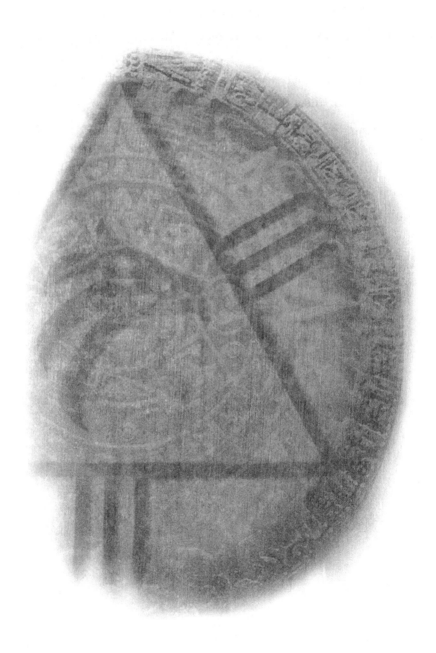

CHAPTER 3

Fill in the Blanks
and Find Your Fortune!

One of most common questions someone asks when they find out you are a **Professional Treasure Hunter or Cacheologist, is: "What does it take to be able to find lost treasure?"** For me the answer is always the same. Even though we use some sophisticated equipment, venture into dangerous environments and brave terrains and situations most people would never venture into, the **KEY** to successful treasure hunting and recovery is (and in my mind will always be) **GREAT RESEARCH**.

GREAT RESREARCH, that's it. Great research is over 90% of the successful treasure hunting process. No special equipment or special physical prowess will ever replace good old fashioned research. Now, for the first time in the history of humanity, we have more research tools and abilities at our fingertips. Yes, sometimes you do have to travel to an area and go to the local records or tax office to find the information you seek, but now most of what you need to research is only as far as your computer.

Think of a computer or your home computer as the most valuable treasure hunting tool you have. My Grandmother died at the age of 103. I would have many conversations with her about history and technology. These conversations gave me a very unique perspective on just how much the world has changed. She marveled at automobiles, air travel and even lived to see fax machines and computers. She was impressed with just how far mankind had come during her day. Now, I think to my days as a child. The use of computers in schools only came to be prevalent once I was leaving high school. Video games to play on your TV came a few years later and then a decade later here come fax machines, and I was amazed when I could call a records office and they could fax me the information the same day and not have to be the standard records request by mail and then wait a couple of weeks to get a response and hard copy in the mail. Then along come bulletin boards, email and eventually the Internet.

Those of you closely familiar with my background know I literally have hundreds of Internet patents and Technology patents, so needless to say, I know the power of technology. When I became in tune and familiar with the Internet and what it would eventually become, I knew it would change the world as we knew it. Back then, I was excited about just being able to see text on a computer screen that someone else wrote. In fact, when I first become involved in technology, there were **NO** pictures on the Internet, no web browsers, no music and it was a rip roaring speed of 2800 baud (for you of those who don't know, compared to today's broadband, G4 or G5 and other new technologies) that was the blinding speed equivalent of my 103 year old grandmother trying to outrun a fighter jet. There just is no comparison – at all!

20

CHAPTER 3 Fill in the Blanks and Find Your Fortune!

Today we literally have the world of information at our fingertips and even powerful countries such as China, Korea, Iraq and Iran cannot keep outside information away from the common populace. The Internet is too big, too free and too powerful to contain or control. No more Dark Ages, where the Church tells you what to think or say. No more learning only the government approved or ruling party version of a story or subject. It is now all wide open for anyone who wants to know. Even the modern news business, TV and print media alike, are almost and I stress **ALMOST** no longer able to contain or spin stories to their own will and sensationalism. Now, with the advent of the Internet, we are getting closer to a revolution of Pure Truth.

I truly believe and stress to my children, now is an amazing time to live in. No, we are not making mad dashes of exploration to jungles or the Poles, as was recent centuries past, but we are now poised to both **REWRITE** and **CORRECT** history and get the message to the entire world. All of this is directly a result of technology being put in the hands of everyone!

So how does this relate to Treasure Hunting? Not too long ago, someone wanting to do research into a long lost treasure would have to visit libraries (several of them since different libraries would carry different books and reference libraries), travel to tax and records offices and send tons of letters requesting information and hope, just hope you got a response, that sometimes only came a month or even, many months later if you were lucky.

Now – as an absolute truth, "Ask and You Shall Receive", all thanks to the Internet.

Since research is 90% of the success of a treasure hunt, and now you have books, public records, military records and every book ever published at your fingertips, you are a master at research and thus can be a master at Treasure Research, and thus Treasure Hunting.

It **IS** as simple as "**FILL IN THE BLANKS AND FIND YOUR FORTUNE**".

This book series is all about the research process. In this state by state book series is treasure of every single type. Hidden Hoards, Caches, Stolen Loot, Lost Mines and Forgotten Fortunes, they are all in between these covers. Whether your favorite type of treasure is in Ghost Towns, buried vaults, in desert sands, in mountain hideaways or at the bottom of the seas, there is treasure here for you to find. All you have to do is fill in the blanks.

Some of the stories inside are loaded with such great facts and clues that all someone has to do is load up in their car, get out at the location with a shovel and dig. Other stories in this book will take research work, some more than others and even better, some of the stories in my various books are **TOTAL** misdirection (only four of them in all my books so don't worry about them being too many of them). Why would I include total horse hockey in any of my books? So you can learn to tell the difference, as the saying goes, "between poop and shoe polish." Kind of hard I know, I am that way. Why would anyone, truly interested in finding lost treasure want fluff and puff? Fluff and Puff is for certain kinds of movies and has no business in the profession of, or for that matter, the recreation of; treasure hunting. Only the hard core facts will pay out.

But you do need to be able to tell the difference between writers' story telling gunk and good, provable treasure clues and leads. So, this book has a little of everything allowing you to hone your skills and hopefully make a fortune.

In my passion of research, my formal team research, and in my schools I use a simple rule called 3x3x3 **C.A.C.H.E.** system.

The acronym of **C.A.C.H.E.** is the actual formula for being wildly successful at cache hunting and recovery.

> **C** – *Consolidate*
>
> **A** – *Authenticate/audit*
>
> **C** – *Cull*
>
> **H** – *History/historical records*
>
> **E** – *Explore/expedition*

C.A.C.H.E is the key to cache. If you take the time to fully understand and employ the steps of the cache acronym, then you could become very successful and very wealthy. It all begins and ends with you and your efforts.

C IS FOR *CONSOLIDATE*

Invariably there are many different versions of any given treasure story. It's the old "telephone game" most of us played as children. Put a classroom of kids in the circle. Whisper a simple to remember phrase or story into the ear of the first student and then have them pass it on in secret to the next student; and so on and so on.

By the time the story comes around back to the teacher, the phrase only minimally resembles the original phrase given to the first student. There four reasons for this phenomenon.

1. **Poor listening skills**
2. **Poor translation skills**
3. **Willful maliciousness**
4. **Human nature**

If you grasp why stories change from person to person and can decipher where they went astray, then you are rapidly and intelligently headed down the path to cache recovery success. It is easy to understand poor listening skills. Most people do not really listen to the actual details of a story. Hundreds and thousands of years ago, when stories were only communicated by word of mouth, people tended to get the story accurate and retell it as told to them. It was a source of pride and was an absolute requirement of the storyteller to get facts flawless. In fact, being the culture's or area's storyteller was a true and noble profession. However, the advent of published works and with the changes in modern society, we have moved storytelling from truth and accurateness to sensationalism, errors, omissions, and bending the truth to suit one's needs.

Poor translation skills not only mean being unable to retell the story as originally told, it also relates to the literal mistranslation of words between cultures and races of people. Such as the common mistranslation of the meaning of the word "church" as it applies to the Bible. For example:

24

CHAPTER 3 Fill in the Blanks and Find Your Fortune!

The English word "church" has various meanings. Webster gives the following definitions for the word church.

1. a building for public Christian worship.
2. a religious service in such a building.
3. (sometimes cap.)
    - A. *the world body of Christian believers; Christendom.*
    - B. *any major division of his body; a Christian denomination.*
4. a Christian congregation.
5. organized religion as distinguished from the state.
6. (cap)
    - A. *The Christian church before the Reformation.*
    - B. *the Roman Catholic Church.*
7. the profession of an ecclesiastic -V. C.
8. to perform a church service of thanksgiving for (a woman after child birth). [Go RI (a)on (DOA) the Lord's house).

Today the word church has a wide variety of meanings from referring to a building to performing a religion service. Although we have an understand the modern use of the word, it is of more significance in understanding the use of the word in the New Testament. It is essential that we understand its original meaning as it was used in New Testament times.

In our English Bible the Greek word, "ekklesia" is translated in most places "church." The word "ekklesia" is found in one hundred and fifteen places in the New Testament. It is translated in English one hundred and thirteen times "church" and the remaining times it is translated "assembly." In classical Greek the word "ekklesia" meant "an assembly of citizens summoned by the crier, the legislative assembly." The word as used in the New Testament is taken from the root of this word, which simply means to "call out." In New Testament times the word was exclusively used to represent a group of people assembled

25

together for a particular cause or purpose. It was never used exclusively to refer to a "religious meeting or group on a building"

An examination of the Greek word "ekklesia" reveals that the word is properly translated into English as the "assembly" or "congregation." It is used to refer to a group of persons that are organized together for a common purpose and who meet together, and was used as early as the 5th Century B.C.

So the word as originally written, shared, and spoken meant one thing, and today we have other completely different meanings. Case in point: there was a time your gay friends meant those who were "happy," not those in "same sex" relationships. So understanding that poor translations skills always come into play is part of the **C.A.C.H.E.** equation.

Now here comes the can of worms, willful maliciousness, and funny how it follows my comments on the church, since one of the most egregious offenders of this in historical terms and culture terms is the institution of the Church. Throughout history (there is that word again history) stories have been modified, augmented, and embellished to reflect favorably on the ruling class, which in most cases was the Church. Now, remember earlier when I mentioned that there is a practice among treasure lore and lost mine writers to willfully omit facts, leads, elements of case and point to hide the actual facts that made lead to a caches discovery? Well, this is most common fact of interference of man when it comes to cache history and lore. Most of the stories get willingly perverted and the truth compromised.

CHAPTER 3 Fill in the Blanks and Find Your Fortune!

This point, now naturally leads us to the nature of Mankind. Man, whether in his DNA or his soul tends to embellish for various reasons, i.e. **(a)** deception, **(b)** personal gain, **(c)** entertainment, **(d)** self-preservation, or; **(e)** self-importance or ego. Let's face it. Most people love attention, love being the center of attention, the topic of the story, and the ironically enough, the bearer of bad news.

Bearer of bad news? Who likes to be the bearer of bad news? Well, think about it. All adventurers and explores are commonly sent off by people who relish telling them **(1)** they are fools, **(2)** chasing a dream, **(3)** wasting their lives, **(4)** will die in the process, and **(5)** will find nothing! Read any account of famous expeditions. This is just a fact of life and the nature of mankind. Most want to be "The Winners" but do not want others "to," win." You have those people in your life right now and I bet you can easily identify them – the dream killers, the moaners and the "you-can't-do-that" crowd. If you have trouble identifying them in your life, announce you are going on a treasure hunt and stand back and watch their individual responses to your announcements. You know these types of people, and they will always reveal themselves!

So how does all of this relate to **CONSOLIDATE**? The first step in mastering **C.A.C.H.E.** is to consolidate everything you can find published, written, noted, and said about the particular cache you are interested in tracking down. This may be 10 items or a thousand items, but consolidate it all in one central place where you can read, reread, research, and study over and over again. Then, with your understanding of the four historical story and legend phenomena, i.e.

1. **Poor listening skills**
2. **Poor translation skills**
3. **Willful maliciousness**
4. **Human nature**

Start shifting through your information so you can get to the **A** in the **C.A.C.H.E.** formula.

A IS FOR *AUTHENTICATE*

Authenticate, as defined by the Merriam-Webster Dictionary is a transitive verb: to prove or serve to prove the authenticity of (authenticate a document).

This is the most important step up to this point. Of all the materials, documents, stories, versions of stories, magazine articles, newspaper clippings, and/or firsthand accounts; you must take steps to determine which of them are authentic. For me, I sometimes make a personal columned grid where I lay out the common threads between each of the versions of the story told. When you lay out the details in a grid and look at them as various points of facts, and they are not crowded and drowned in a sea of letters and words, but presented as bullet points, you can start to recognize patterns. This is one of the very same steps a forensic researcher or F. B. I. profiler starts to create a "description or identity" of a serial killer. The various facts, when arranged properly, can reveal clues; important clues that can be easily overlooked.

But at the very same time you are revealing hidden clues, you are also discriminating fact from fiction. You will be able to identify fancy story telling from factual events that will actually lead to the recovery of the cache. Also during this process you are able to identify the subtle changes over time, writer after writer, story teller after story teller; and be able to discern whether something has been either repeated as true or omitted for one reason or another. If you arrange your **CONSOLIDATION** work and sort them during your **AUTHENTICATION** process chronologically, then you are afforded one more edge: history (which will play a huge role later on as you will read). Comparing stories told or retold by chronological dates, allows you to work your way back to the original source; and the closer to the source the more reliable the information. Remember, detectives don't want to interview the friend of a friend who had a friend that saw the crime occur; they want to get to either the dying victims account or the first person witness accounts. And so do you when it comes to Cacheology. Why? So you can begin the next step in the process, **CULL**.

C IS FOR *CULL*

Here is another transitive verb from Merriam-Webster.
CULL:

1. to select from a group; choose (culled the best passages from the poet's work)
2. to reduce or control the size of (as a herd) by removal (as by hunting) of especially weaker animals; also to hunt or kill (animals) as a means of population control.

Cull, crudely put, is a means of "**CRAP**" control. You need to weigh through the fanciful fabrications and cut to the chase to glean the information that will actually allow you to find the cache. Do not waste your time with useless facts or just decide to pursue a cache hunt with only one story or very little facts. You need fact after verifiable fact. My Professional rule of thumb in going after a particular cache is: three different stories, three different geological anchors, and three verifiable historical accounts or record sources proving the three stories, sources, and individuals involved.

Yes, **3x3x3;** it's my matrix formula of verification and begins the culling process. To give you an example of each: If a particular lost mine story has a particular individual's name attached to it, then verify the existence of the individual. If they found the mine and then somewhere along the way they were killed but told no one about the mine, then there may very well exist a mining claim at the claims office. If it was a huge find of gold and the individual needed sources, tools, and funds to mine the claim, then there will more than likely be an assay record and partnership record and that can verify various points.

If the story of the fantastic claim was written about in the local paper, do a few things: (1) check the papers story against the legend, and (2) check the newspaper writers past stories on the topic. Why the second? Was the newspaper man a "fact reporter" or the papers "fanciful writer"? The first lends more credence to the story, the second means you have to find other sources and not trust this newspaperman's account.

Don't get upset or discouraged if you throw out 80% or more of your collected stories on the cache. That's normal and in fact culling more is normal. Use my proven 3x3x3 method of verifying and culling and you too could be a successful cache hunter. If you do you will make history (there is that word again).

H IS FOR *HISTORY*

History & Historical

Hearsay & Headaches

Hard Work & Head Work

Hysterical & Heartache

Hard fought & Happiness

Each they hunt, hand in hand

The words above have a connection. Each positive begets a positive. Conversely, each negative begets a negative. It is all in how you approach your cache mindset. History is the single most important factor in validating, pinpointing, and recovering a particular cache. If you have history on your side then it is almost as good as having a time machine that will take you back to the very moment in time the cache was deposited.

Whether or not a person means to, they do leave their stamp somewhere along the historical record: censuses, military records, property ownership, shipping manifest and passenger lists. Somewhere the information you seek exists. Searching property records, death and tax records, and information at the local library can go a long way to validating your leads and facts about a certain cache.

If you can go to historic sources and verify the story or lead, and if you can put it into historical context, i.e. three days journey in the 1800s would have been up to a **MAX** of 60 miles, whereby in more recent times, you could have traveled across the whole of the US by car in three days' time. Historical context is paramount. I learned the historical context point the hard way one time when I was looking for an old miner's cabin. I looked and looked for a log cabin but could not find one, and the only broken down wooden structure was a corral. However, the stone miner's cabin was easily found when I corrected for the historical context and location context. A simple change made all the difference in the world.

Adjust your clues according to **HISTORY** and **HISTORICAL CONTEXT** and save yourself a lot of false starts and dead ends.

Now, when reading the stories in this book, please keep in mind the **C.A.C.H.E.** method of detection and validation and see how many clues you can pick out from the stories told and then turn the stories told herein into your very own personal Treasure Case Files, and thus into Lost Treasures that you can find!

CHAPTER 4

How to Build Your
Personal Treasure Case Files

The difference between a treasure story and a treasure case file is the case file has the relevant clues notated, researched, plotted and ready to put to work for the treasure hunter or Cacheologist.

There are certain things that make a case file a real case file. First, of course, is to stick to the 3x3x3: **3 Different Sources** for the same story, from 3 different geological anchors or perspectives with 3 at least three verifiable individuals who were involved in the same treasure story

Now most people ask, "What are the all elements to the 3x3x3 process?" One, there is **NO WAY** to list all the individual elements needed to verify, cross check and re-verify, but there is a starting point. Besides, as any good researcher knows, the more one investigates, the more clues are found that require further investigation. So, you start with the basics and from there the treasure verification matrix expands, up and until the point you have more than enough information to find what you are looking for, and then you have to get off your duff and go out and get it!

As you read the stories inside, you will notice the following check list or table at the end of each treasure story:

```
Who:_____

What:_____

Where:_____

How:_____

Others:_____

Records/Relatives:_____

Tax/Death/Military:_____

Newspapers:_____

      Internet:_____

      Sources:_____

COMMENTS:_____
_____
_____
_____
_____
_____
_____
```

It is this checklist that will enable you to transform these stories into your very own, highly personalized, Treasure Case Files. You might find you want to go research several treasures at once or you may read this book and just select one that meets your personal criteria and likes. From there, you begin the process of making the case file and as with all good detective or forensic research work, you begin with the **WHO, WHAT, WHERE, WHEN** and **HOW**.

CHAPTER 4 How to Build Your Personal Treasure Case Files

In journalism, the **Five Ws** (also known as the Five Ws (and one H), or Six Ws) is a concept in news style, research, and in police investigations that are regarded as basics in information-gathering. It is a formula for getting the "full" story on something. The maxim of the Five Ws (and one H) is that for a report to be considered complete it must answer a checklist of six questions, each of which comprises an interrogative word:

Who? *Who was involved?*

What? *What happened (what's the story)?*

Where? *Where did it take place?*

When? *When did it take place?*

Why? *Why did it happen?*

How? *How did it happen?*

These principles, as with Journalism, Detective work or any forensic research work, also apply to the research work needed to verify, authenticate and locate lost treasures. The principle underlying the maxim is that each question should elicit a factual answer, thus facts necessary to include for a report to be considered complete. Importantly, none of these questions can be answered with a simple "yes" or "no".

Simple yes or no answers, as with any forensic research, does not **VERIFY** or validate any clues for you to follow to find your treasure. You need facts and as many facts as possible. But, the **WHO, WHAT, WHERE, WHEN, WHY** and **HOW** only answer a few of the questions needed to discover the location of a lost treasure. You need to know more. You need to create a map of times, places, people and things, but most important you need to know these facts are reliable. That brings us to the other basic treasure case file questions that need to be asked. On your checklist at the end of each story we have included **OTHERS**.

OTHERS — why others? Simply put, **IF** there were **OTHERS** (additional people involved in the treasure story) then you need to answer the basic questions about all the parties or players involved. When researching one person's background you may come to dead end leads, but when you research everyone involved, it **MOST LIKELY** will give you answers about other people as well and new contacts and links to research out. Simply put, other people involved may give up more clues than the single main player. So **OTHERS** are there to remind you to fully research **ALL** involved and ask yourself "Who else?"

The next items listed are:

RECORDS - RELATIVES - TAX - DEATH - MILITARY

These are self explanatory, but they are reminders of where to look for additional verification and validation information. Are there shipment records? Did they have relatives in the area? Surviving relatives? Death records? Ancestry Records? Did they serve in the Military? The comprehensive search of these types of records, which are available online, will help you find out more about the players and the **OTHERS** and can actually lead to more **OTHERS**. Remember, when it comes to treasure hunting, the more people involved, the more chance of finding clues and leads.

Next on your story checklist comes:

NEWSPAPERS and **WHAT**

In the beginning of this book I talked about how important using the Internet for research is, but when it comes to Newspapers and the articles and stories of the past, most are on the Internet, just not searchable by the Internet standards. That means, you can't just type in words and hope to find old newspaper stories. Most of the old newspaper stories from the 1700's and 1800's are only scanned in as images, and that means the Internet cannot search for the words in them, so when you do a basic search on the Net, you miss most of the newspaper stories. So the **NEWSPAPERS** section is here to remind you to search the areas **NEWSPAPER**. If it happened in Mesa, Arizona then search the Mesa, Arizona Newspaper via various Newspaper Archives. Once you have logged into the archive, then you can search their system remotely and find what you need. Basically as weird as it sounds it's available over the Net but not on the Net. It's on the Newspaper Archive Files.

And that leads to another **WHAT**, simply meaning **IF** you found a newspaper archive story, **WHAT did it say?** Compare it to the other information you collected.

While searching for a $10 Billion, yes, $10 Billion Dollar lost treasure, I read many books written on the topic and tons of accounts, but it was one rare, very rare newspaper article from 1946 that quoted word for word an article from 1810 that gave me the new and valuable information I needed to find the treasures clues.

INTERNET and **SOURCES** is there to remind you to write down and digitally store your Internet Sources for your fact finding. The Internet grows daily and servers go down and websites go out of business hourly. Don't just think you can remember the website you found the information from, chances are you cannot. The volume of information is much too great. So **LOG** your Internet sites and your sources. This means the **WHOLE** web address and not just a name of a website. Again the pages of a web site grow daily and thus pages change daily and server space is made daily by discarding old files. Those files just may be the old story you thought you could go back to.

As a rule of thumb, I do the following on Internet Based sources:

1. **ADD** the **LINK** to your Favorites file in your Web Browser
2. **PRINT** a **HARD COPY** of the information for your hard files
3. **SAVE** a **MIRROR COPY** of the websites pages containing the information you needed and store this to your hard drive. There are many software programs that can mirror image a web page for your computer.
4. **BACK UP! BACK UP! BACK UP ALL YOUR FILES!**

And finally, I have added a **COMMENTS** section so you can add comments on a treasure story as you are inspired and don't lose it by trying to remember to notate it later

READ THIS BOOK WITH A PEN IN HAND!! GO AHEAD AND GET ONE, I WILL WAIT!

And since most people need to be told three times to remember something, well so, here you are. Are you willing to fill in the blanks?

CHAPTER 4 How to Build Your Personal Treasure Case Files

The only thing standing between you and a fortune in lost gold is **RESEARCH.**

If you are willing to fill in the blanks, you can fill your pockets with a fortune.

Got something to write with?

Then let's get going!

CHAPTER 5

How much
UNCLAIMED TREASURE?

OH, I ALMOST forgot one thing. Another question I get asked, actually it's the first question I get asked, is: "Is there really any lost treasure left out there to find?" Instead of my answer in words, how about the spread sheet from my very own personal treasure case files? Have a look at this:

Since I purposefully kept the stories in this book as true to the source as possible, you will come across references to the "value" of the cache, you might see a reference for $60,000 at the time of the story, but remember, that $60,000 in gold in the 1700s is over $5.8 million today in gold weight and could be worth over $34 million in historical value. In fact, a typical treasure chest would hold $64,000,000 in today's dollars and a common child's lunch box would hold over $1,000,000.

To help you relate more to the real value of lost caches, I am including two charts in this chapter. The first is a report published in 1970 detailing the number and approximated value of known lost treasures in each U.S. state. Values are in 1970 dollars. In the second chart, this data has been corrected by our team to account for two things that you need to adjust for: the absolute gold value today as it relates to the gold market price in 1970, and the various case values for the historical values, which are added as upside to the absolute value of the precious metal.

Look up your particular state and see what may be in your very own back yard!

For Reference:

Current PMV is the current value of the precious metal as of the time of this publication, and H/A V is the Historic Artifact and Archaeological/Antiquities value of the find. The H/A V is presented on a 1-2-3 scale where 1 is the worst-case scenario (a minimum value), 2 is the most probable scenario (an average likely value), and 3 is the best-case scenario (the most you're likely to find).

NOTE:

At the time I published these charts gold was at $990.00 per ounce, however at this edit point gold is $1950 per ounce. Therefore, all figures are undervalued and H/A-V values are up over 200%! WOW!

CHART 1:

ESTIMATED VALUES OF UNCLAIMED TREASURES BY STATE
IN 1970 DOLLARS

STATE	Lost Treasures #	VALUE	Sunken Treasures #	VALUE	Lost Mines #	TOTAL Treasure VALUE
Alabama	17	$2,994,000	–	–	–	$2,994,000
Alaska	5	$170,000	2	$4,500,000	1	$4,670,000
Arizona	69	$362,543,500	–	–	91	$36,2543,500
Arkansas	17	$159,362,000	1	$150,000	14	$159,512,000
California	201	$91,513,000	25	$71,040,000	184	$162,553,000
Colorado	63	$144,261,000	–	–	86	$144,261,000
Connecticut	14	$3,165,000	3	$5,000,000	–	$8,165,000
Delaware	7	$500,000	3	$15,600,000	–	$16,100,000
D. C.	1	$25,000	–	–	–	$25,000
Florida	49	$214,137,000	77	$476,054,000	–	$69,0191,000
Georgia	18	$4,364,000	–	–	4	$4,364,000
Hawaii	6	$15,125,000	–	–	–	$15,125,000

STATE	Lost Treasures #	VALUE	Sunken Treasures #	VALUE	Lost Mines #	TOTAL Treasure VALUE
Idaho	33	$2,580,000	1	$25,000	25	$2,605,000
Illinois	14	$4,655,000	_	_	_	$4,655,000
Indiana	6	$1,206,000	_	_	1	$1,206,000
Iowa	8	$232,000	_	_	_	$232,000
Kansas	12	$4,720,000	1	$500,000	1	$5,220,000
Kentucky	12	$8,410,000	_	_	_	$8,410,000
Louisiana	41	$24,175,000	2	$750,000	1	$24,925,000
Maine	33	$1,060,000	1	$35,000	2	$1,095,000
Maryland	11	$2,100,000	_	_	_	$2,100,000
Massachusetts	40	$1,835,000	12	$20,500,000	_	$22,335,000
Michigan	10	$31,055,000	26	$12,202,000	2	$4,3257,000
Minnesota	4	$55,000	_	_	_	$55,000
Mississippi	18	$1,068,000	2	$200,000	1	$1,268,000
Missouri	28	$94,325,000	2	$95,000	5	$94,420,000
Montana	18	$2,622,000	_	_	11	$2,622,000
Nebraska	25	$437,000	1	$100,000	_	$537,000
Nevada	13	$658,000	_	_	35	$658,000
New Hampshire	11	$325,000	_	_	1	$325,000
New Jersey	20	$840,000	6	$11,020,000	_	$11,860,000
New Mexico	75	$1,251,892,000	_	_	44	$1,251,892,000
New York	41	$23,885,000	12	$9,695,000	8	$33,580,000
North Carolina	24	$870,000	8	$3,000,000	3	$3,870,000
North Dakota	7	$330,000	_	_	1	$330,000
Ohio	6	$1,750,000	6	$579,000	1	$2,329,000
Oklahoma	60	$88,150,000	_	_	1	$88,150,000
Oregon	21	$2,921,000	3	$60,000	26	$2,981,000
Pennsylvania	14	$34,981,000	3	$2,200,000	3	$37,181,000
Rhode Island	9	$400,000	1	$250,000	_	$650,000
South Carolina	5	$100,000	_	_	_	$100,000

STATE	Lost Treasures #	Lost Treasures VALUE	Sunken Treasures #	Sunken Treasures VALUE	Lost Mines #	TOTAL Treasure VALUE
South Dakota	15	$1,117,000	_	_	4	$1,117,000
Tennessee	9	$1,560,000	_	_	_	$1,560,000
Texas	190	$299,920,000	39	$40,990,000	47	$340,910,000
Utah	15	$67,233,000	_	_	21	$67,233,000
Vermont	14	$2,319,000	_	_	2	$2,319,000
Virginia	6	$10,081,700	1	$3,500,000	1	$13,581,700
Washington	18	$533,000	_	_	7	$533,000
West Virginia	4	$350,000	_	_	1	$350,000
Wisconsin	12	$1,078,000	5	$395,000	1	$1,473,000
Wyoming	11	$764,000	_	_	10	$764,000
TOTALS	**1380**	**$2,970,752,200**	**243**	**$678,440,000**	**646**	**$3,649,192,200**

CHART 2:

TREASURE VALUES ADJUSTED TO CURRENT DOLLAR VALUES

STATE	CURRENT PMV	H/A V1	H/A V2	H/A V3
Alabama	$87,456,316	$174,912,632	$437,281,579	$874,563,158
Alaska	$136,413,158	$272,826,316	$68,2065,789	$1,364,131,579
Arizona	$10,590,086,447	$21,180,172,895	$52,950,432,237	$105,900,864,474
Arkansas	$4,659,429,474	$9,318,858,947	$23,297,147,368	$46,594,294,737
California	$4,748,258,684	$9,496,517,368	$23,741,293,421	$47,482,586,842
Colorado	$4,213,939,737	$8,427,879,474	$21,069,698,684	$42,139,397,368
Connecticut	$238,503,947	$477,007,895	$1,192,519,737	$2,385,039,474
Delaware	$470,289,474	$940,578,947	$2,351,447,368	$4,702,894,737
D. C.	$730,263	$1,460,526	$3,651,316	$7,302,632
Florida	$20,160,842,368	$40,321,684,737	$100,804,211,842	$201,608,423,684
Georgia	$127,474,737	$254,949,474	$637,373,684	$1,274,747,368
Hawaii	$441,809,211	$883,618,421	$2,209,046,053	$4,418,092,105
Idaho	$76,093,421	$152,186,842	$380,467,105	$760,934,211
Illinois	$135,975,000	$271,950,000	$679,875,000	$1,359,750,000
Indiana	$35,227,895	$70,455,789	$176,139,474	$352,278,947
Iowa	$6,776,842	$13,553,684	$33,884,211	$67,768,421
Kansas	$152,478,947	$304,957,895	$762,394,737	$1,524,789,474
Kentucky	$245,660,526	$491,321,053	$1,228,302,632	$2,456,605,263
Louisiana	$728,072,368	$1,456,144,737	$3,640,361,842	$7,280,723,684
Maine	$31,985,526	$63,971,053	$159,927,632	$319,855,263
Maryland	$61,342,105	$122,684,211	$306,710,526	$613,421,053
Massachusetts	$652,417,105	$1,304,834,211	$3,262,085,526	$6,524,171,053
Michigan	$1,263,559,737	$2,527,119,474	$6,317,798,684	$12,635,597,368
Minnesota	$1,606,579	$3,213,158	$8,032,895	$16,065,789
Mississippi	$37,038,947	$74,077,895	$185,194,737	$370,389,474

TRAVELING BACK IN TIME

HISTORY OF GOLD PRICES SINCE 1793

Gold Price at the time of writing this book is $1950 per ounce

Gold Price % Annual Change   Thursday, April 04, 2013

	USD	AUD	CAD	CHF	CNY	EUR	GBP	INR	JPY
2004	5.4%	1.4%	-2.1%	-3.5%	13.6%	-3.1%	-2.4%	0.5%	3.7%
2005	20.0%	28.9%	15.4%	37.8%	21.3%	36.7%	33.0%	24.2%	37.6%
2006	23.0%	12.6%	23.0%	14.2%	18.7%	10.6%	8.3%	20.8%	24.4%
2007	30.9%	18.3%	12.1%	21.7%	23.3%	18.4%	29.2%	16.5%	22.9%
2008	5.6%	31.3%	30.1%	-0.1%	-2.4%	10.5%	43.2%	28.8%	-14.4%
2009	23.4%	-3.0%	5.9%	20.1%	23.6%	20.7%	12.7%	19.3%	26.8%
2010	27.1%	13.3%	21.3%	15.4%	22.8%	37.1%	31.4%	22.3%	11.4%
2011	10.1%	10.2%	13.5%	11.2%	5.9%	14.2%	10.5%	31.1%	4.5%
2012	7.0%	5.4%	4.3%	4.2%	6.2%	4.9%	2.2%	10.3%	20.7%
2013	-7.4%	-7.5%	-5.6%	-4.6%	-8.0%	-5.3%	-1.0%	-7.1%	2.6%
Average	14.5%	11.1%	11.8%	11.6%	12.5%	14.5%	16.7%	16.7%	14.0%

goldprice.org

GOLD PRICES 2012 back to 1793

Gold Price at the time of writing this book is $1950 per ounce

2012 - $1,810

2011 - $1,950.00   2010 - $1,024.53

2009 - $972.35	1990 - $386.20	1971 - $44.60	1952 - $38.70
2008 - $871.96	1989 - $401.00	1970 - $38.90	1951 - $40.00
2007 - $695.39	1988 - $410.15	1969 - $41.00	1950 - $40.25
2006 - $603.46	1987 - $486.50	1968 - $43.50	1949 - $40.50
2005 - $444.74	1986 - $390.90	1967 - $35.50	1948 - $42.00
2004 - $409.72	1985 - $327.00	1966 - $35.40	1947 - $43.00
2003 - $363.38	1984 - $309.00	1965 - $35.50	1946 - $38.25
2002 - $309.73	1983 - $380.00	1964 - $35.35	1945 - $37.25
2001 - $271.04	1982 - $447.00	1963 - $35.25	1944 - $36.25
2000 - $279.11	1981 - $400.00	1962 - $35.35	1943 - $36.50
1999 - $290.25	1980 - $594.90	1961 - $35.50	1942 - $35.50
1998 - $288.70	1979 - $459.00	1960 - $36.50	1941 - $35.50
1997 - $287.05	1978 - $208.10	1959 - $45.25	1940 - $34.50
1996 - $369.00	1977 - $161.10	1958 - $35.25	1939 - $35.00
1995 - $387.00	1976 - $133.77	1957 - $35.25	1938 - $35.00
1994 - $383.25	1975 - $139.29	1956 - $35.20	1937 - $35.00
1993 - $391.75	1974 - $183.77	1955 - $35.15	1936 - $35.00
1992 - $333.00	1973 - $106.48	1954 - $35.25	1935 - $35.00
1991 - $353.15	1972 - $63.84	1953 - $35.50	1934 - $35.00

1933 - $32.32	1897 - $20.67	1861 - $20.67	1825 - $19.39
1932 - $20.67	1896 - $20.67	1860 - $20.67	1824 - $19.39
1931 - $20.67	1895 - $20.67	1859 - $20.67	1823 - $19.39
1930 - $20.67	1894 - $20.67	1858 - $20.67	1822 - $19.39
1929 - $20.67	1893 - $20.67	1857 - $20.71	1821 - $19.39
1928 - $20.67	1892 - $20.67	1856 - $20.67	1820 - $19.39
1927 - $20.67	1891 - $20.67	1855 - $20.67	1819 - $19.39
1926 - $20.67	1890 - $20.67	1854 - $20.67	1818 - $19.39
1925 - $20.67	1889 - $20.67	1853 - $20.67	1817 - $19.39
1924 - $20.67	1888 - $20.67	1852 - $20.67	1816 - $19.84
1923 - $20.67	1887 - $20.67	1851 - $20.67	1815 - $22.16
1922 - $20.67	1886 - $20.67	1850 - $20.67	1814 - $21.79
1921 - $20.67	1885 - $20.67	1849 - $20.67	1813 - $19.39
1920 - $20.67	1884 - $20.67	1848 - $20.67	1812 - $19.39
1919 - $20.67	1883 - $20.67	1847 - $20.67	1811 - $19.39
1918 - $20.67	1882 - $20.67	1846 - $20.67	1810 - $19.39
1917 - $20.67	1881 - $20.67	1845 - $20.67	1809 - $19.39
1916 - $20.67	1880 - $20.67	1844 - $20.67	1808 - $19.39
1915 - $20.67	1879 - $20.67	1943 - $20.67	1807 - $19.39
1914 - $20.67	1878 - $20.69	1842 - $20.69	1806 - $19.39
1913 - $20.67	1877 - $21.25	1841 - $20.67	1805 - $19.39
1912 - $20.67	1876 - $22.30	1840 - $20.73	1804 - $19.39
1911 - $20.67	1875 - $23.54	1839 - $20.73	1803 - $19.39
1910 - $20.67	1874 - $23.09	1838 - $20.73	1802 - $19.39
1909 - $20.67	1873 - $22.74	1837 - $21.60	1801 - $19.39
1908 - $20.67	1872 - $23.19	1836 - $20.69	1800 - $19.39
1907 - $20.67	1871 - $22.59	1835 - $20.69	1799 - $19.39
1906 - $20.67	1870 - $22.88	1834 - $20.69	1798 - $19.39
1905 - $20.67	1869 - $25.11	1833 - $19.39	1797 - $19.39
1904 - $20.67	1868 - $27.95	1832 - $19.39	1796 - $19.39
1903 - $20.67	1867 - $27.86	1831 - $19.39	1795 - $19.39
1902 - $20.67	1866 - $28.26	1830 - $19.39	1794 - $19.39
1901 - $20.67	1865 - $30.22	1829 - $19.39	1793 - $19.39
1900 - $20.67	1864 - $47.02	1828 - $19.39	
1899 - $20.67	1863 - $31.23	1827 - $19.39	
1898 - $20.67	1862 - $27.35	1826 - $19.39	

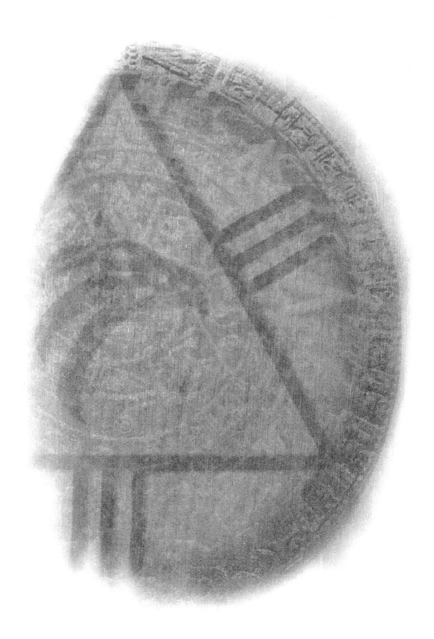

CHAPTER 6

Case Files: IOWA

Columbus Junction

In the early 1900s, train robberies were still rampant across the Midwest. Between the existence of gangs, Indians, and individuals just trying to jump on the crime bandwagon; it is a wonder that anybody was safe on the railroads at all. During one particularly harrowing period of time, it was estimated that thirty percent of all the railroad links were either robbed at gunpoint or hijacked altogether.

Columbus Junction, Iowa was one of the unfortunate cities that had to experience this type of crime for many years. Because of these robberies and the ensuing gun battles, many buried treasures were left scattered throughout the county. Some of these hoards of buried gold are still lost today. Such is the case for the following two examples.

In 1904, a train was boarded while slowing down after crossing the gang-planted explosive devices on the tracks. They were primitive materials and nothing as sophisticated as we might see today, but the mini explosion did catch the conductor's attention. Once the gang was on board, it was only a matter of money moments before the safe was opened and the train's coffers were out $30,000 in gold and silver coins. The bandits then buried the loot between Letts and Columbus Junction, and were off for their next raid. They were killed before having the chance to return for their loot.

In 1934, a plumbing contractor was digging to install a septic tank at a home near Letts, Iowa when he struck a rock hard area in his hole. Bewildered, he continued digging until he found a leather sack with $10,000 of gold coins inside. Since outlaws typically buried their stolen loot in more than one location, this was believed to be part of the Columbus Junction train robbery funds. The remaining $20,000 has never been found.

In 1910, close to Whisky Hollow, another train was relieved of its funds as well, although by a different method. Two masked robbers uncoupled the engine and express car from the rest of the train while in station, six miles south of Muscatine, Iowa. They then hijacked the engine car and drove the conductor and a guard through the tracks in Iowa until eventually stopping near Columbus Junction. There, the bandits took the loot out of the express car and left the victims tied up and alone with their empty train. They too, were in the vicinity of Columbus Junction when they buried the gold and agreed to come back when their pursuers had long finished searching for them. The total amount of this cache was $50,000. They never returned, presumably due to the short life expectancy of most bandits, and the gold remains hidden in the plains of Columbus Junction.

The total value of these two missing caches of $70,000 in gold is $4.375m.

Who:_____

What:_____

Where:_____

How:_____

Others:_____

Records/Relatives:_____

Tax/Death/Military:_____

Newspapers:_____

    Internet:_____

    Sources:_____

COMMENTS:_____

_____

_____

_____

_____

_____

_____

_____

_____

_____

_____

_____

_____

_____

NOTES

_____
_____
_____
_____
_____
_____
_____
_____
_____
_____
_____
_____
_____
_____
_____
_____
_____
_____
_____
_____
_____

The Wheeler Ranch

The life of a prospector in the late 1800s was as dangerous as it was exciting. If you managed to survive the tough life of working all day while enduring the outside elements, you often risked your life simply by finding the elusive gold prize. Word traveled quickly so prospectors had to be careful who they shared their success stories with. Thomas Nelson was one such fortune hunter. Nelson amassed a small fortune through his lucky prospecting skills in the Black Hills and also through his clever poker playing.

It is reported that one night, while in his room at the Wheeler Ranch, he had removed his stash of coins from their hiding place in order to take a tally of his wealth. While counting his coins, a fellow worker at the ranch came into his room and witnessed his bounty. It only took a matter of days for the other locals in Cerro Gordo County, Iowa to learn of the reported fortune.

Like any wise individual with wealth in those days, Nelson searched for a safe location to hide his earnings. He searched for several days and nights until he found the perfect site. There was a secluded spot near a grove of trees in the area between the Wheeler Ranch and the horseshoe bend at the Winnebago River. Nelson knew the landmarks in this area quite well so he was sure he would be able to later find his stash when it was time.

Perhaps Nelson's memory was not as keen as he had once thought; because when he returned just a few days later to retrieve his money, he was unable to find the stash. It is reported that Nelson spent the next decade fervently searching for his fortune. He searched so haphazardly and frantically that he was eventually charged for trespassing on the owner's land. Nelson seemingly accepted his fate in the early 1900s when he moved to the Mason City area of Alaska to search for new gold.

Rumors say Nelson was followed on the night he buried his money and that is why he never found it even after years of searching. Others believe Nelson dug so deep in order to hide the treasure that he simply never dug far enough to hit the payload. While small sums of money have been found in the area over the years, nothing amounting to Nelson's reported wealth has ever been claimed.

The Wheeler Ranch is located in Odebolt, Iowa and has existed as one piece of land since its nine sections were purchased by H. C. Wheeler in 1871. It is currently the most wealthy and largest farm in Iowa. This land was purchased from the Iowa Railroad Land Company for three dollars an acre, but Wheeler received a discount because of the size of his purchase. He had made a fortune in business enterprises in California and through money speculation during the Civil War.

Who:_____

What:_____

Where:_____

How:_____

Others:_____

Records/Relatives:_____

Tax/Death/Military:_____

Newspapers:_____

    Internet:_____

    Sources:_____

COMMENTS:_____

_____

_____

_____

_____

_____

_____

_____

_____

_____

_____

_____

_____

NOTES

Black Hawk

From the early 1800's to 1832 the Sac and Fox Indian tribes were embattled with white settlers in the Black Hawk War. The war was over territory in Iowa which was eventually purchased from the Indians for $30,000 and additional annual payments of $20,000 payable over the next thirty years. Another treaty was agreed upon in 1833 for a payment of $1,000 a year over the next 25 years. There were numerous other arrangements made between the white settlers and Indian tribes.

The confusing part of the arrangements was the fact the Indians had little to no value for the payments they received. As familiar inhabitants of the land, the tribes were self sustaining and survived on their own agriculture, hunting, and traditions. Money only had value if you needed to purchase something from the settlers rather than procure the item yourself. The tribes were fond of the weaponry the settlers brought with them, namely rifles and also their alcohol.

Much distrust existed between the Indians and their white neighbors. Many believed they were being setup with the payments and hid the payments they received. It is believed much has been hidden in the southern and eastern parts of Iowa since these were the areas with the greatest native population. Proof of these hidden payments was discovered when a letter dated June 25, 1828 gave descriptive information to the location of hidden money. The information was found in the old Bonnifield log cabin near Fairfield when the oldest building at the time was being demolished. The letter made mention of the money being hidden not at the point marked A, but rather near the middle. The author shares how he was given information from an Indian, but believes the complete truth was not told and the value of the money to be more than $10,000.

A legendary tale told through the years in this area supports the claims of the letter. Legend has it three Indians were chosen to hide the payments. In the event something happened to one of the diggers, the other two would be able to locate the payments. The creators of the plan did not count on all three Indians dying before sharing information on where the money was hidden. Black Hawk himself is buried on the Northwest Quarter of Section Two, Township 70, Range 12, in Davis County, Iowa. Black Hawk lived most of his life near this land and rarely ventured away during his latter years. It is believed he refused to travel because he did not want to leave his post guarding his money. He was very specific with his burial instructions also. Perhaps he was planning to continue his watch even after death.

It is estimated that, if found, the coins would be almost too high to even calculate their value in today's market, because of their extreme rarity.

Who:_____

What:_____

Where:_____

How:_____

Others:_____

Records/Relatives:_____

Tax/Death/Military:_____

Newspapers:_____

Internet:_____

Sources:_____

COMMENTS:_____

_____

_____

_____

_____

_____

_____

_____

_____

_____

_____

_____

_____

NOTES

_____
_____
_____
_____
_____
_____
_____
_____
_____
_____
_____
_____
_____
_____
_____
_____
_____
_____
_____

Beebeetown

The average driver passing through the tiny rural hamlet of Beebeetown, Iowa, could sneeze and completely miss it. The construction of Interstate 80 just to the south most likely means Beebeetown will continue its long, inglorious fading into the dusty pages of history. Estimates of the local population have dropped as low as 25 people. Still, those few citizens are very proud of their little neck of the woods. They're proud of their ramshackle school building, the century-old frame houses, and the legend of buried treasure that stubbornly persists to this day.

Over 100 years ago, long before highways criss-crossed rural Iowa, people had very few options for transporting valuable items from one town to another. Trains had become more common, but the tracks did not run through all areas. A heavy strongbox containing currency or precious metals could not be carried on horseback, so stagecoaches became the transportation of choice for banks trying to send money between distant locations.

One such strongbox, containing a considerable sum of gold owned by Wells Fargo, fell into the care of two rough and ready stagecoach drivers. Hauling gold through wild outlaw country was not a job for the faint of heart, and these men were tough and always ready to answer an attack. But they were also smart and valued their jobs very highly. They believed their primary mission was to protect their cargo, and they constantly looked for new ways to keep gold out of criminal hands.

On this particular trip, the two drivers set out for Council Bluffs, Iowa, just over the border from Omaha, Nebraska, with the Wells Fargo strongbox safely stowed. At one of the stagecoach stations along the road, they struck up a conversation with some of the locals, who related some unpleasant rumors of highwaymen being active further up the trail, probably near Beebeetown. Although the drivers were not certain the rumors were true, they still thought long and hard about their options. Diverting east or west might mean missing the bandits around Beebeetown, but the additional distance could add days to their journey. And of course, they had no guarantee there weren't bandits on the other routes either.

So the men made their decision, made their peace, and set out for the penultimate leg of the journey. Three miles outside of Beebeetown, the drivers made their last known contact and related that they would most likely be held up further down the road. But they had a plan. Heading south, they knew the trail branched off on to Fred Beebee's land, and the men knew of the perfect place to bury their cargo for safekeeping, while they went ahead and scouted for highwaymen.

As the drivers expected, armed men assaulted them not much farther down the road. Finding no gold, the outlaws grew angry and gunned down the coachmen in cold blood. The story goes that the criminals never learned of the gold's location, and though treasure hunters have gone searching, nothing has yet been recovered.

Who:_____

What:_____

Where:_____

How:_____

Others:_____

Records/Relatives:_____

Tax/Death/Military:_____

Newspapers:_____

    Internet:_____

    Sources:_____

COMMENTS:_____

_____

_____

_____

_____

_____

_____

_____

_____

_____

_____

_____

_____

_____

NOTES

Fort Mckay

Payroll shipments during the tumultuous and precarious Native America conflicts in America were some of the most feared tasks for a soldier to handle. The deliveries became a hit or miss type of operation. But until the Indian nation was pacified, these attacks would continue.

The largest shipment of payroll gold to the military occurred at Fort McKay, Iowa in 1830. Four bulging sacks of pure ore were delivered from St. Louis and were to be distributed to the soldiers who had been fervently protecting the Fort and all the surrounding areas from Indian attacks. Colonel Taylor accepted the payroll but made a plan to hide the funds until the current week-long battle with the Native American tribes was completed and they were in the process of retreat. It was currently a highly dangerous and conflicted time around the fort and he didn't want all of his men traveling home with their wages, open to broad attacks from every angle.

The Colonel chose four brave and successful soldiers to take the entire payroll and, when they had found a location they deemed safe enough, bury the gold completely. They each carried one of the cumbersome and weighty sacks. The men understood the grave danger and importance of this mission, but felt well-qualified to complete the task without incident. They left with stern faces, their eyes conducting scans of the area at every moment. The four soldiers never made it back to Fort McKay.

The men had basically walked into a trap; the Indians were lying in wait behind the trees, watching the entire departure process. As soon as the soldiers were far enough away from the Fort to be invisible, the Indians ambushed the party and conducted a massive attack again them. All four soldiers were killed and left naked and scalped at the scene. The Indians buried the money at the site and danced their tribal ritual dance around the scene before leaving for their next attack.

Colonel Taylor sent a search party out for the missing soldiers who returned within a day with the devastating news. They were sent back to look for the gold, but after digging sporadically for the remainder of the week, nothing was recovered.

The four sacks of gold are still buried under the ground at the former Fort McKay site, in northeastern Iowa. The fort was originally named Fort Shelby, but was renamed by the British commanders who took over its control in the early part of the nineteenth century. The fort was overtaken time and time again by Indians throughout the 1800s, and the commanders eventually had to surrender and burn the entire fort to the ground to make their escape through cover of smoke. The property was located in Iowa, north of Prairie du Chien, Wisconsin, on the banks of the Mississippi River.

The four sacks of gold are estimated to be worth over one million dollars today,

Who:_____

What:_____

Where:_____

How:_____

Others:_____

Records/Relatives:_____

Tax/Death/Military:_____

Newspapers:_____

     Internet:_____

     Sources:_____

COMMENTS:_____

_____

_____

_____

_____

_____

_____

_____

_____

_____

_____

_____

_____

_____

NOTES

Extra Notes

Extra Notes

Extra Notes

www.ExpeditionHistory.org   Copy 2014 JHP

www.TREASUREFORCE.com

Extra Notes

Extra Notes

www.ExpeditionHistory.org   Copy 2014 JHP   www.TREASUREFORCE.com

Extra Notes

Extra Notes

_____

_____

_____

_____

_____

_____

_____

_____

_____

_____

_____

_____

_____

_____

_____

_____

_____

_____

_____

_____

_____

_____

_____

Extra Notes

Extra Notes

CHAPTER 7

The Increasing Value
of Precious Metals

At the beginning of the book, I shared with you how gold is ever increasing in value and how a lost treasure cache worth $60,000 long ago is now worth over $5.8 million dollars. To complete your precious metals education and help you find the real value of the treasure you see. I offer the following overview on the ever increasing value of precious metals.

Precious metals are metals that occur naturally and are usually rare. Gold, silver and platinum are the most well known examples of precious metals, but there are others such as palladium, rhodium, osmium, and iridium. All are important industrial commodities, and some are used in designing jewelry.

Throughout history, gold, silver and platinum has been used by various cultures to create currency, thus assigning a monetary value to these precious metals. While seldom used in currency anymore, these precious metals have continued to rank highly as an investment commodity sought after by institutional and private investors alike.

Demand for gold, silver and platinum remains high, pushing prices to record highs. In the last decade, gold and silver prices have climbed, more than 300 percent, while platinum has

87

increased over 185 percent. A favored asset class, these precious metals remain attractive to investors because of the stability and longevity offered, particularly during difficult political or economic times.

A review of the long history of gold, silver, and platinum supports the premise that these precious metals are likely to remain strong over the near to intermediate future, thus deserving of closer consideration.

GOLD

Pure gold is exceptionally heavy. It has a distinctive gold-yellow color with a metallic sheen. It is very compliant, flexible and easily cut. Native gold however usually contains 10 to 15 percent silver. Gold that contains a silver content that is more than 20 percent is called electrum. When combined with silver or copper, the color of gold changes to a whiter or orange color depending on the other metal involved. Besides being used to create money and jewelry, it has high electrical and thermal conductivity making it popular for various industrial uses.

The ancient Egyptians left behind one of the earliest and most expansive gold legacies of all times. Gold was believed to be a divine and indestructible metal associated with the sun. The Egyptians appear to have begun mining gold prior to 2000 BC, as there are hieroglyphics describing gold, dating back to 2600 BC.

This precious metal also played a dominant role in Greek and Roman civilizations. As these empires expanded, so did their quest to increase gold reserves. Mining activities dramatically increased throughout the regions (central Europe, Asia, etc.) under their control. Even after the reach of these vast empires weakened, gold mining activities continued to grow, bringing wealth to the leaders of newly formed countries.

Discoveries of new gold sources around the world, and technological advances in mining and processing gold, contributed to the continued growth in global gold production throughout the centuries. Today, gold is extracted from mines on every continent except Antarctica, where mining is forbidden.

Global Demand

The global demand for gold remains high, especially in East Asia, the Indian sub-continent, and the Middle East. These regions account for about 70 percent of the world's demand for gold. Fifty-five percent of total demand can be attributed specifically to India, Italy, Turkey, China, and U.S. experts project that demand will remain particularly high in China and India for the foreseeable future.

The World Gold Council estimates that the total volume of gold mined since its discovery is approximately 158,000 tons, of which about 65 percent has been excavated since 1950. Over the last five years, average annual production levels have remained stable at 2,485 tons[1].

At the end of 2008, there was approximately 163,000 tons of above ground gold stocks. Stock levels of gold held for making jewelry were the highest, comprising 51 percent of the total amount of above ground gold stocks. The official sector (i.e., governments) held 18 percent of these reserves, and private investment holdings accounted for another 17 percent.

While proportions vary from country to country, estimates suggest that most individual governments hold, on average, 10 percent of their official reserves in gold. Central banks and supranational organizations such as the IMF currently hold just

---

[1] Retrieved from the World Gold Council website,
www.invest.gold.org/sites/en/why_gold/demand_and_supply/ on 4/5/2010.

under one-fifth of the global above ground stocks of gold as reserve assets, according to the World Gold Council.

In recent years, the demand for gold as an investment has increased significantly. The World Gold Council finds that investment demand for gold has shown the strongest growth. Between 2003 and 2008, investment demand increased approximately 412 percent.

Global Market

Gold is traded 24-hours a day around the world in most major financial centers. However, London has long dominated for centuries as a major gold center, involved in the setting of gold prices. Even to this day, the prices set twice daily by the London Bullion Market Association (LBMA), which represents the wholesale over-the-counter market for gold and silver, serves as a benchmark for other institutions around the world.

The troy ounce is the traditional unit of weight used for precious metals. All references to ounces mean troy ounces in the bullion market. When trading gold, a trading unit is represented as one fine troy ounce. The value of a gold coin or bar depends on the weight of the gold contained in the item. Purity of gold is measured in carats with pure gold being 24-carat gold. It is also expressed in terms of fineness or parts per thousand. For example, 18-carat gold would be 750 fine or 75 percent gold.

Precious metal prices are not simply set based on supply and demand. It is a bit more complicated. The supply of gold is always increasing since it is not a consumable product. Even when used in making jewelry, gold is recoverable and able to maintain its value, based on the amount of gold that went into creating that product. Gold's inability to be consumed has therefore added to the development of a rather sophisticated commodity trading market that fixes prices based not on supply and demand, but on numerous contributing variables.

Throughout history, gold prices have remained relatively stable for long periods. For instance, the U.S. government has only changed its gold prices four times since 1792. One of the most significant changes came in 1973, when the government eliminated the Gold Standard, allowing the dollar to float freely, no longer tying it to gold[2].

The price of gold over the last three decades is illustrated below in this graph based on COMEX futures prices.

Gold prices remained relatively modest and stable until 1974. At that time, the U.S. government lifted a forty-year ban, once again allowing its citizens to buy and hold gold bullion and coin. Prices continued to move upward in 1975 when the public sales of gold stocks in the U.S. were initiated. Gold has continued on a steady upward trend ever since. For a more comprehensive history of gold prices in the U.S. from 1793 to 2009, refer to Appendix A.

SILVER

Unlike gold, silver is seldom found in nature in a pure form. Native silver usually contains varying amounts of gold, copper, mercury, arsenic, or antimony The color of silver ranges from silver white to grey and sometimes even black, if tarnished. Like gold, it is fairly yielding and pliable, and serves as a good electrical and thermal conductor.

Since ancient times, silver has been used for a variety of purposes, many more practical in use than gold. For early travelers on long voyagers, containers made of silver were prized because they kept wine, milk, vinegar, and water fresher. For leaders like Croesus

---

[2] Watt, J., Gold and silver throughout history, page 77.

(560-546 BC), the king of Lydia, silver would serve as an official coinage. Since those earlier times, silver has been used for everything from batteries and water purification to dental applications and mirrors.

According to the website, Silver Insights, total worldwide silver production has amounted to 40 billion ounces. Of that total, 65 percent has been produced since 1900[3]. Today, the three main demand drivers for silver are jewelry and silverware, industrial uses, and photography. Combined, these three categories account for 95 percent of annual silver consumption.

COINAGE

For centuries, silver coins were an essential part of national and international trade for numerous countries throughout the world. In the U.S., silver coins remained in circulation until the supply of silver could no longer meet the demand for coins. At that time, the face value of the coins actually fell below its bullion (meltdown value). By 1965, the government had eliminated silver from quarters and dimes, and the silver in half dollars was reduced to 40 percent. Today, silver is used only in bullion, commemorative, and proof coins in the U.S. Mexico is the only country currently using silver in its circulating coinage[4].

Interestingly, over the last ten years, several countries, including the U.S., Canada, and Mexico have again begun issuing pure silver coins with nominal face values, sold at a small premium over bullion value (not face value). For example, the U.S. Mint issues a 999-fine Silver Eagle bullion coin (a one-ounce bullion coin with a face value of $1). Over 165 million of these coins have been sold since 1986.

---

[3] Covers the period of 3000 BC to 2008.

[4] The Silver Institute, retrieved from www.silverinstitute.org/store_value.php, on April 5, 2010.

Silver Market

Like gold, silver is traded 24/7 around the world. London serves as a major center for the world's physical silver trade, while the **COMEX** division of the New York Mercantile Exchange in the U.S. dominates the paper contract market for silver. Silver prices are available from several sources. The **LBMA**, which sets physical gold prices, also sets silver prices. **COMEX** determines prevailing spot prices for silver, and Handy & Harman, a precious metals company, publishes an updated price once each working day.

Silver prices have ridden a rollercoaster throughout much of the twentieth century, as illustrated in the chart below. Events affecting silver prices included the U.S. government's decision in 1965, to eliminate the use of silver from all coins, except the half dollar, and its withdrawal of all silver coins from circulation in 1967. An attempt to corner the silver market in 1979-1980 led to a rise in prices, and then a subsequent fall to more realistic levels.

Yearly Average Price of Silver Since 1950

Source: The Silver Institute

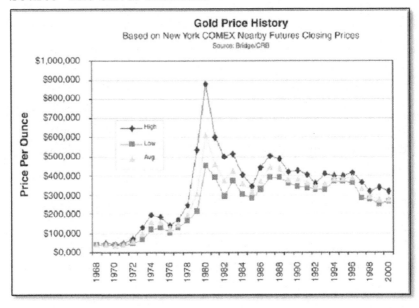

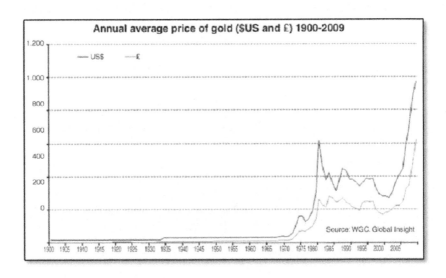

CHAPTER 7 The Increasing Value of Precious Metals

Silver prices have, for the most part moved steadily upward over the last ten years. However, in 2009, a weak U.S. dollar drove the price of most precious medals downward briefly. Silver was especially hit hard. It has since showed strong signs of rebounding.

10 Year Silver Price History

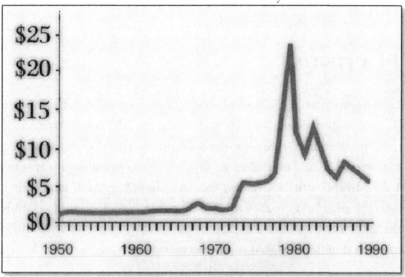

10-Year Silver Price History

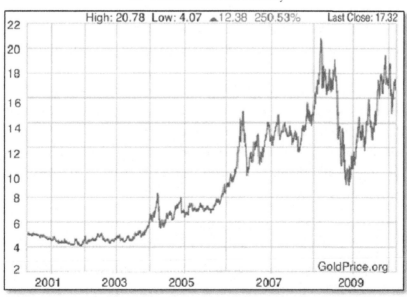

Appendix B provides additional information on silver including a 650-year graph of silver prices and the silver/gold ratio from 1344 to 2004. An annual price history for silver from 1840 to mid-2009 is also available.

Silver is traded as one troy ounce, of which a minimum of 999 parts in every 1,000 must be silver.

PLATINUM

In comparison to gold and silver, platinum is a relative newcomer. Archaeological evidence indicates that pre-Colombian Americans near modern-day Ecuador used platinum to produce artifacts. Europeans however did not "discover" the metal until around 1557. It did not appear to be that highly prized when first discovered, as the Spaniards mining for gold in Columbia during the 17th century considered it a nuisance because it apparently interfered with their gold mining activities.

By the 18th century, platinum had gained in popularity after it was found to have several industrial uses. Jewelers and goldsmiths also weighed in, finding the metal attractive and malleable for making expensive cutlery, watch-chains and coat buttons. Once jewelers were able to use high-temperature torches to mold platinum in the 19th century, jewelry using platinum began to show up with greater frequency. Today, as one of the densest metals known, its high melting point and temperature stability has made it useful for a variety of industrial applications ranging from chemical processing, electronics, and glass, to petroleum, automotive catalysts, and fuel cells.

While gold and silver has a long pedigree of being used for currency, platinum was not utilized for making coinage until 1828, when Russia began turning out platinum coins. Over an 18-year period, Russia minted over 500,000 ounces of platinum and were

96

instrumental in showing the world that platinum was not just a commodity, but that it held monetary value like gold and silver.

Supply & Demand

Platinum is not an easy metal to produce or mine. It takes approximately 10 tons of ore just to produce a single ounce of platinum. The extraction process is dangerous, costly, and time consuming. It can take up to six months for miners to extract 10 tons of ore. In addition, unlike most other precious metals, platinum deposits are found mostly in only two main areas of the world: South Africa and Russia. Thus, any disruption to mining production because of labor strikes or political instability can dramatically drive prices through the roof, as seen in 1986 when work stopped in the Impala Platinum Holdings mines in South Africa.

Because of these difficulties and expenses, only about 7 million ounces of new platinum reaches the world market each year. This is less than 10 percent of annual gold production, and less than one percent of annual world silver production. It has been estimated that if all platinum were mined today, it would only fill a room measuring less than 25 cubic feet (the size of a crate used to ship a car)[5].

Unlike gold, over 50 percent of all platinum produced is consumed, particularly in industrial applications. If mining activities were to cease today, there would only be enough above ground platinum reserves to last a year, whereas if the same scenario existed for gold, there would be enough reserves to last twenty-five years.

As of 2009, the drivers for platinum demand were jewelry, auto catalyst and industrial. Platinum for investment purposes only

---

[5] Platinum – History & Investment, Azom.com.

made up a small portion of the total market, as illustrated in the graph below.

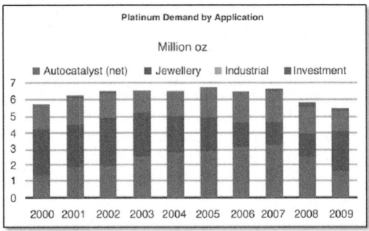

Platinum Market

Platinum is the scarcest of the precious metals and its price indicates this. As demand for platinum has continued to grow, and supplies remain relatively fixed, the price of platinum has continued to rise, even after accounting for inflation. Nick Barisheff of The Millennium Bullion Fund noted that platinum prices from 2000 to 2006 rose 190 percent, far surpassing silver's 150 percent and gold's 120 percent increase[6].

Source: Financial Sense

---

[6] Taken from the article Platinum – Dark Horse, Bright Future.

The London Platinum and Palladium Market (LPPM) fixes prices between market-making members of the LPPM twice daily. Johnson Matthey PGM, the world's leading authority on platinum metal groups, generally sets base prices five times a day for wholesale quantities of platinum group metals, based on market offer prices throughout the world. The Tokyo Commodities Exchange is the primary exchange for trading platinum futures; however, they are also listed on the New York Mercantile Exchange.

INVESTING IN PRECIOUS METALS

Economic Hedge

For thousands of years, precious metals have served as a way for investors to preserve wealth. Unlike stocks, bonds, and currencies, precious metals are not tied to a mere promise to perform, or the whim of any particular government, if it decides to fire up the printing press and flood the market with additional currency to cover growing debt levels[7]. Precious metals during times of worsening economic conditions tend to appreciate. That is why they are often referred to as crisis commodities. It is common for many people to buy gold when the dollar is at risk and inflation is rising.

When doubt grows regarding the stability of a financial system and market volatility appears to enjoy free range, gold remains a strong investment, as it has no counterparty risks. In other words, it is a tangible asset not dependent on another's promise.

Precious metals retain their value, and investors often find that even if they purchase these metals at peak prices, they are often far better off than those investors who funneled money into real

---

[7] An example of fiat money, i.e. money that the government declares to be legal tender although it cannot be converted into standard specie.

estate and the stock market at their highest price points. In 2008, for instance, stocks lost 30 to 70 percent of their value, while gold increased approximately 5 percent. More surprising to many was that gold's volatility remained relatively low compared to many of the other asset classes.

Inflation Protection

When investors include precious metals in their portfolios, they gain unparalleled inflation protection over the long-term. Nick Barisheff in The Next Economic Crisis: Spiraling Inflation illustrates this point with the following scenario:

> *In 1971, you could buy a car for 66 ounces of gold, buy a house for 703 ounces and "buy" the Dow for 25 ounces. Today, the same amount of gold will purchase several cars and several houses, while you can buy the Dow with less than half as much gold. This trend is not only expected to continue but to dramatically accelerate because, as Merrill Lynch economist David Rosenberg points out, the new growth engine for the economy is government spending[8].*

Several studies also support the position that precious metals such as gold provide a meaningful hedge against expected inflation. One study looking at daily returns between 1976 and 2004 found that precious metals had particularly high hedging capabilities during periods of abnormal stock market volatility. Researchers concluded that investment portfolios that contained precious metals significantly outperformed all equity portfolios over that period.[9]

Over the previous decade, precious metals have consistently performed better than stocks and bonds. This is illustrated best in

---

[8] The Next Economic Crisis, Spiraling Inflation, Part 2.

[9] Do Precious Metals Shine? An Investment Perspective

the figure provided below prepared by the Bouillon Management Group (2009).[10]

Precious metals are the most negatively correlated asset class to stocks and bonds, as illustrated by a thirty-year study compiled by Ibbotson Associates.[11] Simply put, as stocks and bonds fall in price, precious metals tend to rise, and vice versa. Ibbotson Associates may have summed up the role of precious metal investing best when it concluded, "during periods of stress [precious metals bullion] provided returns when they were needed most."

Precious Metal vs. Major Investment Indices

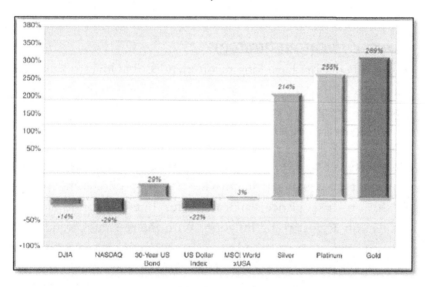

---

[10] Preserve Your Wealth With Precious Metals by Barisheff

[11] Preserve Your Wealth with Precious Metals by Hamlin

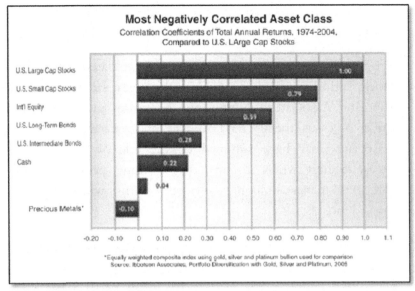

Asset Allocation Strategy

Financial advisors have long recommended that investors allocate anywhere from 10 to 20 percent of their investment portfolio in precious metals. This of course depends on an individual's investment strategy.

As stocks continue to ride a rollercoaster, investors need to seek out asset classes that will provide the best purchasing power. Cash, on first glance, appears safe, but does not provide protection against rising inflation. With interest rates trending at around zero percent, bonds are not attractive as interest rates have nowhere to go but up. That may be why many seasoned investors continue to look to precious metals like gold, silver and platinum.

During periods of economic downturn, investors place particular emphasis on rebalancing their portfolios, but surprisingly, they often ignore the benefits of adding precious metals. This oversight could potentially expose investors to the harsh losses associated with economic downturns, financial crises and inflation.

Precious Metal Investment Vehicles

Investors interested in precious metals have several investment options available to them. They can choose to purchase coins, bullion, certificates, pooled accounts, exchange traded funds (ETFs), and even mining stocks. The figure below, provided by Bullion Management Group, shows the different investment vehicles based on inherent risk.[12] The best option will largely depend on the investment goals and risk tolerance of each investor.

Precious Metal Investment Vehicles

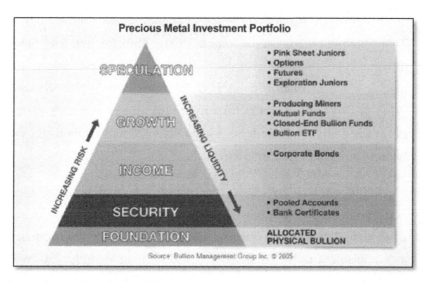

An overview of a few of the more popular precious metal investment options are overviewed below:

---

[12] The Next Economic Crisis, Spiraling Inflation, Part 2.

Bullions Coins and Bars

The earliest known coins were called cobs and were cut by hand from bars of silver and gold, and then hammered between handmade dies. Three different civilizations in Asia Minor, India and China, sometime between the 7th and 6th century BC, were among the first to use coins for financial transactions. Since then, gold and silver coins have served as continued examples of commodity money.[13]

Currently, governments around the world issue a wide range of bullion coins. It is important to remember that bullion coins should not be confused with commemorative or numismatic coins. The value for numismatic coins is based on their rarity, design, and finish and not the amount of gold content.

To capitalize on price movements in the market, investors have historically used bullion coins. For investment purposes, the market value of bullion coins is determined by two factors: the value of fine gold content and a premium (markup), which varies between coins and dealers. Generally, premiums tend to be higher for smaller denominations.

Small bullion bars are bars that weigh less than 1000 grams. Ninety-four accredited bar manufacturers and brands, producing more than 400 types of standard gold bars in twenty-six countries are available on the market. Typically, a small gold bar will contain a minimum of 99.5 percent fine gold.

Many investors prefer physical bullion and coins because they receive exclusive title when purchased. These investment vehicles

---

[13] Commodity money is one of three types of money commonly used. The other two types are representative and fiat. With commodity money, the value of the coins is directly tied to the amount of precious metal contained.

remain relatively safe and have the lowest associated risk when compared to other investment options. However, as with any investment vehicle, there are potential drawbacks. For instance, if you buy coins or bullion, you need to have a place to store (or hide) it, which requires additional costs such as insurance and storage fees. Additionally, it will not pay interest or create additional wealth, unless you periodically sell, which will result in transaction costs and possibly taxes. Furthermore, if you decide to sell your pieces, you will need to pay a company to test its authenticity. If you do not want to take actual ownership of your gold or silver, you can use a certified vault holder, which would also eliminate the need for authenticity testing when you decide to sell, but you would still incur holding fees.

Under the Sea

Treasure hunters are not the only group interested in what lies beneath the oceans blue. Precious metal investors have turned an eye to the seas as well. Experts estimate that one-third of the world's gold is lost beneath the sea along with jewels, silver, and valuable and historical artifacts. Gold does not rust, therefore gold artifacts[14] recovered from shipwrecks that have been buried for thousands of years are still as bright and shiny as the day they were made.

Many established dealers of shipwreck coins and artifacts remain confident that ingots, artifacts and treasure coins may experience regular market difficulties, but that they never go to zero. Scott Travers, author of Top 88 Coins to Buy & Sell believes the best time to buy treasure coins is not at their original offering price,

---

[14] Ocean treasure hunting dream team gets celeb Captain

but when they are brought to market at a significant discount. After the excitement fades, the high prices tend to as well.[15]

Many experts believe that the supply of gold yielded from these underwater sites may come with an expiration date. A United Nation's report estimates that there are over 3 million shipwrecks on the ocean floor. While this may seem like a lot, the rate of discovery suggests the supply is diminishing. Archaeologist Don Keith of the Discover Research Institute at the Corpus Christi Museum of Science and History estimates that half the shipwreck sites that will be found, have already been found. Additionally, at the current rate of discovery, he believes all wrecks off the coasts of Australia, Europe, Great Britain, Canada, the U.S., and the Caribbean Islands will be discovered in the next 30 years.[16]

Mining Stocks

Investors also turn to mining stocks when thinking of diversifying their portfolios. Unfortunately, this option may not provide as much asset protection as assumed. While mining stocks often track the price of precious metals, there are historical examples (1987), when mining stocks declined by greater margins than what the equity market did, even though the price of some precious metals rose.[17] Stocks can, as illustrated frequently by the market, be quite volatile.

Another concern with mining stocks is that they are not plentiful in regards to some precious metals like platinum. For instance, the only major producers are South African stocks such as Impala

---

[15] Navigating Shipwreck Coins

[16] Insider: Profiteers on the High Seas

[17] Platinum – Dark Horse, Bright Future.

Platinum (AGL SJ), Anglo-American Platinum (IMP SJ), and Lonmin Plc (LON SJ).

Mutual Funds & ETFs

Precious metal mutual funds work well for investors who may not want to actually handle physical gold or silver. Mutual funds pay dividends while investors gain equity in the companies that produce the precious metals. Exchange Traded Funds (ETFs), while backed by physical gold, are also attractive because the investor can buy precious metals without taking physical delivery of it. However, like stocks, they can be volatile, and are often dependent on fund managers making the right decisions regarding which stocks should be included in the funds.

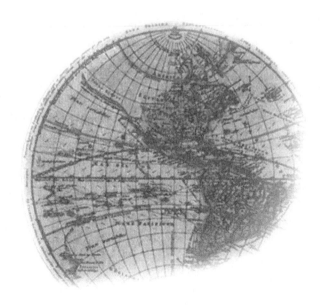

OUTLOOK

Prices for many precious metals continue to rise, and many economists and industry followers expect this trend to continue in the near future. among those, suggesting prices will climb even further is Scotia Mocatta. In its Precious Metal Forecast 2010, the global leader in precious metals trading and finance made the following predictions:

- The outlook for gold will remain bullish, as it continues to provide a hedge against weakness in fiat currencies and possible further turmoil in the markets.

- Silver still has good upside potential. Prices are suggested to range between $13 and $75 per ounce.

- Investor interest in platinum is likely to continue, as economic recovery is expected to spur demand once again. Platinum is projected to trade in the $1,900 to $2,500 per ounce range in the next few years.

CONCLUSION

Precious metals have a long history both as an industrial commodity and as an investment commodity. While many investors turn to precious metals during economic downturns as a safe haven, precious metals are a sound investment during both good and bad times as illustrated by its rather extensive and illustrious history.

APPENDIX A:

GOLD PRICES 2012 Back to 1793
Gold Price at the time of writing this book is $1950 per ounce

2012 - $1,810

Year	Price	Year	Price	Year	Price
2011	$1950.00	1976	$133.77	1941	$35.50
2010	$1,024.53	1975	$139.29	1940	$34.50
2009	$972.35	1974	$183.77	1939	$35.00
2008	$871.96	1973	$106.48	1938	$35.00
2007	$695.39	1972	$63.84	1937	$35.00
2006	$603.46	1971	$44.60	1936	$35.00
2005	$444.74	1970	$38.90	1935	$35.00
2004	$409.72	1969	$41.00	1934	$35.00
2003	$363.38	1968	$43.50	1933	$32.32
2002	$309.73	1967	$35.50	1932	$20.67
2001	$271.04	1966	$35.40	1931	$20.67
2000	$279.11	1965	$35.50	1930	$20.67
1999	$290.25	1964	$35.35	1929	$20.67
1998	$288.70	1963	$35.25	1928	$20.67
1997	$287.05	1962	$35.35	1927	$20.67
1996	$369.00	1961	$35.50	1926	$20.67
1995	$387.00	1960	$36.50	1925	$20.67
1994	$383.25	1959	$45.25	1924	$20.67
1993	$391.75	1958	$35.25	1923	$20.67
1992	$333.00	1957	$35.25	1922	$20.67
1991	$353.15	1956	$35.20	1921	$20.67
1990	$386.20	1955	$35.15	1920	$20.67
1989	$401.00	1954	$35.25	1919	$20.67
1988	$410.15	1953	$35.50	1918	$20.67
1987	$486.50	1952	$38.70	1917	$20.67
1986	$390.90	1951	$40.00	1916	$20.67
1985	$327.00	1950	$40.25	1915	$20.67
1984	$309.00	1949	$40.50	1914	$20.67
1983	$380.00	1948	$42.00	1913	$20.67
1982	$447.00	1947	$43.00	1912	$20.67
1981	$400.00	1946	$38.25	1911	$20.67
1980	$594.90	1945	$37.25	1910	$20.67
1979	$459.00	1944	$36.25	1909	$20.67
1978	$208.10	1943	$36.50	1908	$20.67
1977	$161.10	1942	$35.50	1907	$20.67

Year	Value	Year	Value	Year	Value
1906	$20.67	1868	$27.86	1830	$19.39
1905	$20.67	1867	$27.86	1829	$19.39
1904	$20.67	1866	$28.26	1828	$19.39
1903	$20.67	1865	$30.22	1827	$19.39
1902	$20.67	1864	$47.02	1826	$19.39
1901	$20.67	1863	$31.23	1825	$19.39
1900	$20.67	1862	$27.35	1824	$19.39
1899	$20.67	1861	$20.67	1823	$19.39
1898	$20.67	1860	$20.67	1822	$19.39
1897	$20.67	1859	$20.67	1821	$19.39
1896	$20.67	1858	$20.67	1820	$19.39
1895	$20.67	1857	$20.71	1819	$19.39
1894	$20.67	1856	$20.67	1818	$19.39
1893	$20.67	1855	$20.67	1817	$19.39
1892	$20.67	1854	$20.67	1816	$19.84
1891	$20.67	1853	$20.67	1815	$22.16
1890	$20.67	1852	$20.67	1814	$21.79
1889	$20.67	1851	$20.67	1813	$19.39
1888	$20.67	1850	$20.67	1812	$19.39
1887	$20.67	1849	$20.67	1811	$19.39
1886	$20.67	1848	$20.67	1810	$19.39
1885	$20.67	1847	$20.67	1809	$19.39
1884	$20.67	1846	$20.67	1808	$19.39
1883	$20.67	1845	$20.67	1807	$19.39
1882	$20.67	1844	$20.67	1806	$19.39
1881	$20.67	1943	$20.67	1805	$19.39
1880	$20.67	1842	$20.69	1804	$19.39
1879	$20.67	1841	$20.67	1803	$19.39
1878	$20.69	1840	$20.73	1802	$19.39
1877	$21.25	1839	$20.73	1801	$19.39
1876	$22.30	1838	$20.73	1800	$19.39
1875	$23.54	1837	$21.60	1799	$19.39
1874	$23.09	1836	$20.69	1798	$19.39
1873	$22.74	1835	$20.69	1797	$19.39
1872	$23.19	1834	$20.69	1796	$19.39
1871	$22.59	1833	$19.39	1795	$19.39
1870	$22.88	1832	$19.39	1794	$19.39
1869	$25.11	1831	$19.39	1793	$19.39

APPENDIX B:

650 Year Look at Prices

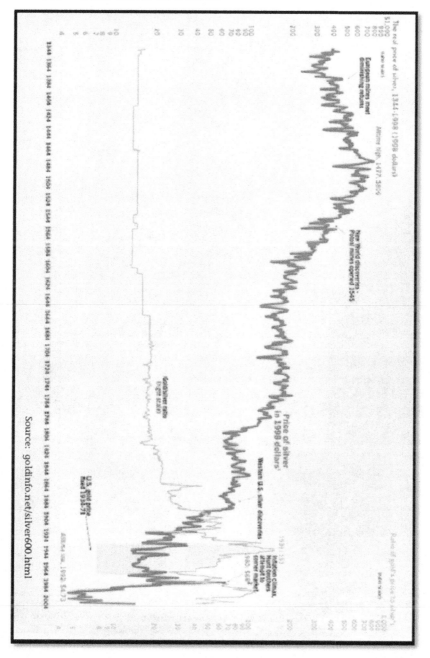

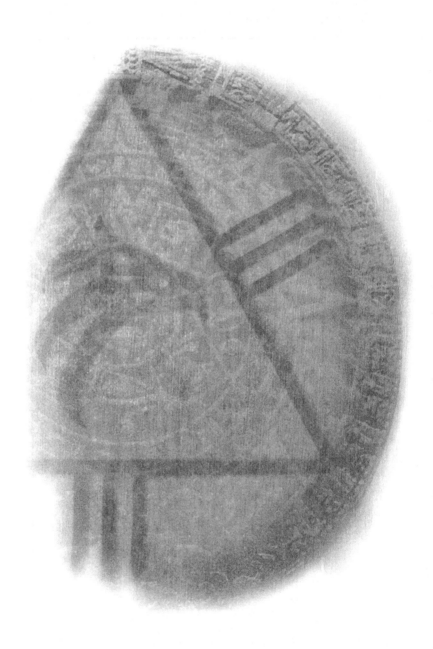

CHAPTER 8

Photographic Journal of a Recent Cache Expedition

Photographic Journal of a Recent Cache Expedition

COMMANDER

Commander explaining the mission back story for **EXPEDITION HISTORY**™ viewers

EXPEDITION HISTORY™ gets to visit and explore some of the most beautiful and wild places around the globe.

COMMANDER

Commander pointing to the Team how these rocks actually mark a hidden gold mine's camouflaged entrance. The Team found the hidden entrance in the center of three triangulated markers just like these.

The Team documents the find and presses forward.

COMMANDER

Commander getting ready to lead the way through a mountain canyon. Just a quarter of a mile after this photo Commander faces off with a Gila monster and a huge rattlesnake.

Commander and one member of his personal team, his dog Angel.

ALPHA TEAM

Beast brings an intensity to the **EXPEDITION HISTORY**™ Team.

Beast inside a magnificent water-worn canyon. Look at solid rock wall formations worn smooth by the flow of water over millions of years.

ALPHA TEAM

When you gotta go, you gotta go.

The Beast inspecting the surrounding rocks for geological clues.

ALPHA TEAM

Beast heads out to scout the area.

Beast and Logi, on an unexpected mission to try to recover the body of a hiker involved in a fatal fall from a canyon's edge. The Team had to hike in 5 miles to search the entire canyon and its creek path for signs of the body.

ALPHA TEAM

Logi of **EXPEDITION HISTORY**™ doing her pre-flight inspection and preparation to go on an air recon mission over the high desert.

Logi coordinates a route for other Team members.

ALPHA TEAM

Logi sets up a parameter inside the cave while Beast scouts ahead.

Logi scouts near a ravine for clues.

ALPHA TEAM

Logi communicates with the underwater Team.

Alpha Team prepares to enter the deepest part of the cave system.

BRAVO TEAM

Does every Puerto Rican strike the "Captain Morgan" pose naturally?

Now Oro says a little prayer for great weather before launching on his flight recon mission.

BRAVO TEAM

No matter the conditions or environment, Team members MUST wear protective body armor when they go in the field.

Oro performing his pre-flight checks as he gets ready to conduct an air recon mission over the Lost History's suspected location.

130

BRAVO TEAM

Oro communicates to base camp after hearing of a discovery Delta Team had made.

Oro and Flex, suited up and heading out on a mission that took them on a 5-mile hike over a rocky stream bed through canyons. Imagine a hike over the course of five miles that was the equivalent of walking on top of bowling balls the whole way.

BRAVO TEAM

Flex trekking through a gold-encrusted canyon.

Flex shows off her namesake.

BRAVO TEAM

Flex doing reconnaissance trying to pinpoint the location of a suspected landmark.

Flex and Gizmo prepping for a mission.

134

BRAVO TEAM

Commander and Flex take a brief rest as Joker does the immediate area recon.

Bravo Team discussing its next steps. At this moment they were on a search and rescue mission to find the body of a possible deceased backpacker that was suspected lost in the area where the treasure hunt was being conducted.

135

DELTA TEAM

Joker has a disagreement with Commander on how the team should proceed on and new discovery.

Joker likes his new ride a little too much.

DELTA TEAM

Traversing through a cave can be very dangerous, Joker is a highly trained expert.

Everyone has duties when establishing base camp. Here Joker tried to hammer a tent spike into the rocky desert floor.

138

DELTA TEAM

Joker documents the discoveries he makes in the field as they happen.

Delta team's Joker and Gizmo during a mission.

DELTA TEAM

In this photo, Gizmo is getting ready for a Mountain Recon expedition. Color coded equipment makes it easy for Team Members to get ready for a Mission on a moment's notice.

Gizmo taking recon photographs in high definition formats. This is the very sequence of photographs she took that lead us to the treasure's historic location. The teams often documents sites and possible sources of treasure with high-definition photography.

DELTA TEAM

Gizmo appears to have found something.

Gizmo climbs up the ravine to get a better look at a landmark that is suppose to lead to a treasure.

DELTA TEAM

Laughter and joking keeps the teams strong and together.

BASE CAMP

Sherlock in the Tactical Command Center.

Commander going over the current operation with Sherlock.

BASE CAMP

Joker and Sherlock discuss how to proceed on a mission.

Sherlock prepares for the mission.

EXPEDITION HISTORY

SARGE

Base Camp Manager - Base Camp Manager, Diesel Mechanic, Electrician, Camp Cook, Supply Sergeant, Maintenance Supervisor, Weapons Expert, Camp Manager, Wild Animal Expert, Grumpy Old Man

TREASUREFORCE

BASE CAMP

Sarge is an all around Cook-Mechanic: Mr. Fix-It and Camp Manager.

Sarge, getting his first order of business started in base camp. Food and coffee!

BASE CAMP

"If you scratch my back, I'll scratch yours!" Being a Team player is paramount to treasure success!

Let a piece of vital equipment like this generator go down, and you can be sure Sarge can fix it.

FLEET

Anywhere the **EXPEDITION HISTORY**™ convoy is stopped along U. S. Highways, it draws a crowd. Each **EXPEDITION HISTORY**™ vehicle has a specific mission and tactical purpose and function.

When the **EXPEDITION HISTORY**™ Team travels it is in a military convoy formation. Each vehicle is in constant contact with the other vehicles. This way the entire convoy can watch out for each vehicle in case of emergencies while on the road.

FLEET

Commander leading the Convoy through Mexico.

Convoy about to arrive at Base Camp.

FLEET

Every mission has equipment failures; this time it was a dead battery at base camp.

Flat number 5 of 9! Yes, 1 mission with 9 flats total.

BASE CAMP

EXPEDITION HISTORY™ color-codes everything, even down to the tents, to ensure efficient and professional base camp management. A disorganized base camp usually leads to poor expedition results.

High wind storms demolished based camp four times. If you look closely Joker is trying to hold the mess tent together while Beast and Sarge try to find bracing materials.

BASE CAMP

Commander coming to the rescue..

The team prepares for the days mission.

BASE CAMP

Commander and Joker checking the various mounted cameras that document and record each mission.

Joker and Commander accidentally run over a large rattlesnake. Nothing goes to waste. Guess what's for dinner in Base Camp?

BASE CAMP

Each team member is monitored using a real time two-way GPS tracking system. Here Joker helps Oro suit up and get his systems synced.

Trying to stay ahead of a looming snow storm while making their way out of the high country. See the storm brewing in the sky above them.

BASE CAMP

This is Angel. She is 13 years old and lives for missions.

This is Blue. He can't wait to get out and get to work.

CHAPTER 9
Various Cacheology
Equipment Samples

Of all the equipment we get to use in history hunting, my absolute favorite is the helicopter. You can go through any terrain, get a great sense of the area and they are a joy to use and fly.

With modern advancements in ultra-light flight, aircraft like this Powered Parachute are of tremendous value. Where a helicopter can be $1,000 an hour to operate, a Powered Parachute can be operated for less than $20 an hour.

This Powered Parachute is Logi's; she's one of the pilots and the Team Logistics Officer.

Modified Deuce and a Half Military Trailer. Designed to carry equipment across rough terrain.

Small, highly mobile tactical 4x4s are very important to any mountain, wilderness, or desert expedition.

Originally a Medical Attack Vehicle or M. A. V. , and serves as a Mobile Command Center.

The best custom 4x4 Expedition Vehicle made, a **Quigley Custom 4x4.**

F. L. I. R. : FLIRs (Forward Looking Infrared) use detection of thermal energy to create the "picture" assembled for the video output; they can be used to help pilots and drivers steer their vehicles at night and in fog, or detect warm objects against a cold background when it is completely dark (such as a cloudy, moonless night). The wavelength of infrared that FLIRs detects differs significantly from that of night vision, which operates in the visible light and near infrared ranges (0.4 to 1.0 micrometers).

Remote Sensing Cameras are used for area recon.

Unmanned Aerial Vehicle: This one is called the DraganFlyer X6. It is a remote unmanned helicopter that can record video and photos and be used from remote distances to recon or film a target Treasure Area. The team uses U. A. V. s for preliminary site recon from the Air.

This is what is used to find shipwrecks, a
Proton Magnetometer. The proton magnetometer, also known as the proton
precession magnetometer (PPM), uses the
principle of Earth's field nuclear magnetic
resonance (EFNMR) to measure very small variations in the Earth's magnetic field, allowing ferrous objects on land and at sea to be detected. They are used in land-based archaeology to map the positions of demolished walls and buildings and at sea to locate wrecked ships for recreational diving.

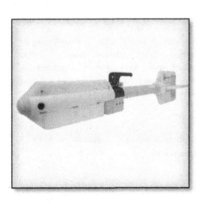

CHAPTER 9 Various Cacheology Equipment Samples

A Hovercraft is a great way to get in and out of remote areas for History Hunting. A hovercraft (air-cushion vehicle, ACV) is a craft capable of traveling over surfaces while supported by a cushion of slow moving, high-pressure air, which is ejected against the surface below and contained within a "skirt. " Although supported by air, a hovercraft is not considered an aircraft. Hovercrafts are used throughout the world as specialized transports. They can also be used after a natural disaster for emergency purposes. Because they are supported by a cushion of air, hovercraft are unique among all other forms of ground transportation in their ability to travel equally well over land, ice, and water. Small hovercraft are used for sport, or passenger service, while giant hovercraft have civilian and military applications, and are used to transport cars, tanks, and large

There are many instances that neither man nor vehicle can get into a specific area safely, such as a cave. In those instances TreasureForce utilizes various forms of robots or U. M. V. 's, "UnManned Vehicles." UMV's can go where team members cannot and can explore to make sure an area is safe before a team sortie is attempted.

165

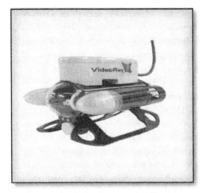

This is an R. O. V. A remotely operated vehicle (ROV) is a tethered underwater robot. An ROV may sometimes be called a remotely operated underwater vehicle to distinguish it from remote control vehicles operating on land or in the air. ROVs are unoccupied, highly maneuverable, and operated by a person aboard a vessel. They are linked to the ship by a tether (sometimes referred to as an umbilical cable), a group of cables that carry electrical power, video and data signals back and forth between the operator and the vehicle.

There are different kinds of metal detectors. This one is specifically designed to pinpoint a find and narrow down the search

This is the type of helmet the team uses when inside caves. Always make sure you have the right equipment for the Expedition.

Having no equipment or even the wrong equipment can mean you die in the field.

CHAPTER 9 Various Cacheology Equipment Samples

EXPEDITION HISTORY™ team members always carry extra water even on the simplest of missions. This is a hydration backpack. Water is stored in an internal bladder and fed to the expedition member via a watering tube. These are invaluable on any and every mission.

These are common HD 1080p cameras used to record missions in the field. They are extremely rugged and capture the action of the mission and help treasure hunters go back and review footage for clues they missed while in the field. These cameras can be mounted to helmets, bodies, vehicles, and tripods in the field.

P. O. V. camera (point of view camera). This camera (as show above) has key features like a playback screen, remotes to save memory and extend battery life; in addition they have all important external microphone port for doing the audio documentation of the expedition along with the video footage.

A field POV and documentation camera is best mounted on a field helmet for the best camera shots and picture stability. Shoulder mounts and wrist mounts produce footage that can move too much, thus producing poor images.

P. O. V. cameras are easily attached – along with extra batteries and memory – to field MOLLE vest. MOLLE is an acronym which means Modular Lightweight Load-carrying Equipment. It is the current load-bearing system that is employed by the United States Army.

When in the field the team members wear protective body armor. Shown above are various samples. Simple body armor can mean the difference in a life or death situation in the field.

This is a simple rope and rappelling harness, which is essential for scaling canyons and mountains in search of treasure.

Rappelling harness can be in a backpack form for carrying additional gear and supplies.

These are two must-haves for the field: An emergency first aid and a trauma kit. Not having one on hand can mean the death of a team member.

This is an individual emergency locator. The SPOT Satellite GPS Messenger provides a vital line of communication with friends and family when you want it and emergency assistance when you need it. Using satellite technology, SPOT works virtually anywhere in the world, even where cell phones don't – all with the push of a button. When in the field, this is what you "don't leave

Commander likes to say his team members hunt gold like hound dogs track blood; all the while Commander is tracking his team exactly like dogs. As Commander says "Hey, you have to use what works!"

CHAPTER 9 Various Cacheology Equipment Samples

Since there is no consumer two-way GPOS tracking device that allows for tracking in real time without the use of Internet connections, the team uses real hunting dog trackers. Each team member can see exactly where and how far away their other team members are. Team members do not leave base camp without this tracking system. These can mean the difference between living and dying when in the extreme wilderness. The team learned the hard way to use this type of technology after almost losing a team member to

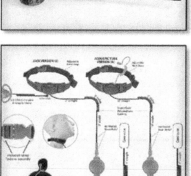

When climbing mountains, scaling canyons or hiking across rough terrain, Expedition History team members need their hands free to maneuver. To make sure we are in constant contact and have our hands free we utilize military throat microphones in the field.

The **EXPEDITION HISTORY**™ Team redefines adventure.

TreasureForce travels by land, sea and sky.

CHAPTER 10

Cacheology Treasure Examples

Cacheology Terrain and Treasure Samples

Ancient mine entrance in reverse. Never go in a mine alone or without protective gear. In fact, abandoned mines claim more lives than falls or wrecks combined.

An ancient tomb entrance looking out.

Cacheology Terrain and Treasure Samples

Ancient storage tomb. Notice the
rolling slab door.

Ancient symbols in stone.

Ancient man's footprints captured in soft ground that became fossilized.

Cacheology Terrain and Treasure Samples

Typical storage tomb and rocky mine entrance.

Abandoned mine entrance in area prone to flooding. Vertical shafts entrances like this one are far more dangerous than horizontal openings like the photo above.

Cacheology Terrain and Treasure Samples

Chichen Nitza in Mexico.

Angkor Wat statues in modern Cambodia.

Cacheology Terrain and Treasure Samples

Impressive stone temple.

Central American stepped pyramid

Cacheology Terrain and Treasure Samples

Asian stele.

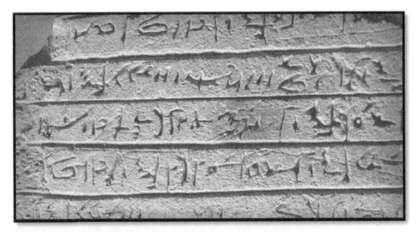

Ancient Stele – Stele is a stone or wooden slab, generally taller than it is wide, erected for funerals or commemorative purposes, most usually decorated with the names and titles of the deceased or living inscribed, carved in relief or painted onto the slab. It can also be used as territorial markers to delineate land ownership.

Cacheology Terrain and Treasure Samples

Mayan stele.

Asian Stele.

Ancient Stele.

Cacheology Terrain and Treasure Samples

This is an example of Nazi gold. The Nazis stole and subsequently hid several billion dollars worth of gold.

Gold has an absolute value in precious metals weight, but gold like this that is marked and molded and important to Archaeology can be worth 10 to 40 times its weight in precious metal. For example, a small Spanish gold bar with $2,000 of gold weight is easily worth $40,000 on the collectors' market.

Cacheology Terrain and Treasure Samples

Theses artifacts from Central America are known as tumbagas. Tumbaga was the name given by Spaniards to a non-specific alloy of gold and copper which they found in widespread use in pre-Columbian Mesoamerica and South America.

Ancient gold coin hoard found.

Cacheology Terrain and Treasure Samples

Solid gold minted ancient coins.

Gold doubloon. This is an original treasure find from an unnamed wreck found off Cuba. The piece dates from about 1630 from the reign of King Philipe IV, from the Sevilla Mint in Spain.

Cacheology Terrain and Treasure Samples

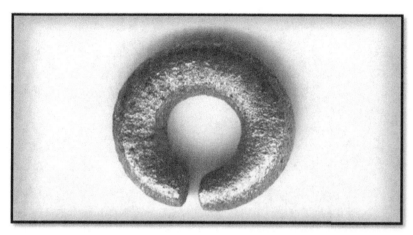

This gold ring is actually a form of ancient money called "ring money."

Another doubloon sample.

Cacheology Terrain and Treasure Samples

Doubloon sample.

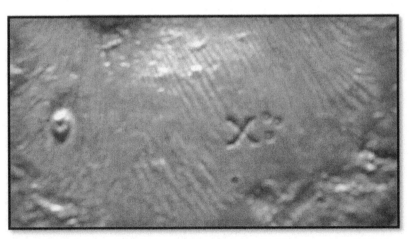

Pay close attention to finds to see if they carry a Spanish mark as shown above. These are more valuable.

186

Cacheology Terrain and Treasure Samples

Silver doubloon sample.

Would you know what this was if you found it on the ocean floor? Seems simple, but one could easily bring $500,000 if you find the right one.

CHAPTER 11

Amazing Cacheology Locations

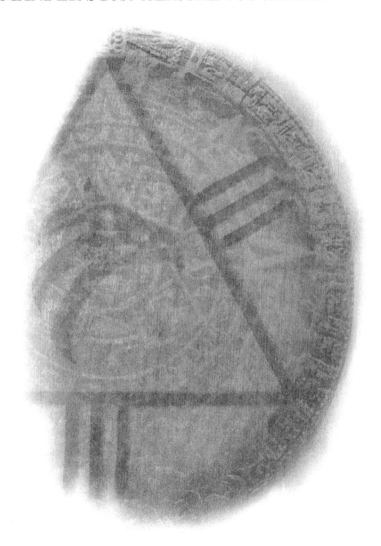

Amazing Cacheology Locations

Amazing Cacheology Locations

Amazing Cacheology Locations

CHAPTER 12

Mother Nature's Treasures

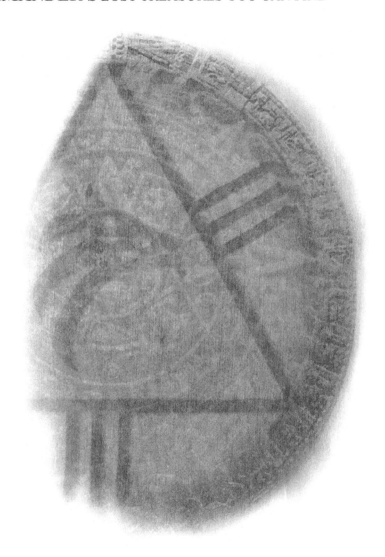

Mother Nature's Treasures

Gold can be over $1,800 an ounce, but did you know middle-of-the-road-quality diamonds can bring over $200,000 an ounce?

These are diamond formations called Macels.

Mother Nature's Treasures

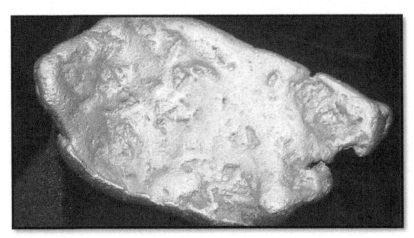

This is a typical gold nugget. A gold nugget can be anywhere between 12-karat and 22-karat pure right out of the ground.

This is what gold looks like when recovered after hundreds, even thousands of years. Gold, both buried and lost in water, does not tarnish over time. How would you like a find like this?

198

Mother Nature's Treasures

Another sample of gold in crystal.

Gold nuggets can also take on a crystal-like formation naturally.

Mother Nature's Treasures

This is an emerald in its natural form. The clearer, greener and larger the crystal
the more valuable an emerald is. Emeralds are more valuable than diamonds.

Looks like a ruby in color and shape, but this is a priceless American native
treasure, Bixbite. Bixbite is only found in Utah and is actually a Red Emerald.
America is loaded with treasures.

Mother Nature's Treasures

Diamonds in their rough form can also be perfectly round like marbles.

This huge diamond is the traditional pyramid upon pyramid shape, called octahedron.

Gold commonly occurs in crystal. Find crystal start looking for gold.

What would you do as a history hunter if you came across a skeleton? Is this modern or ancient?

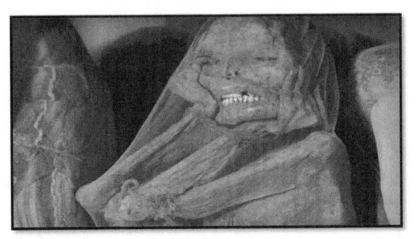

When you find a skeleton or mummy like the ones above, what do you do? Nothing but call the State's or Government's Antiquities authorities. Disturbing these can land you in jail.

CHAPTER 13

More "Commander" Treasure Books

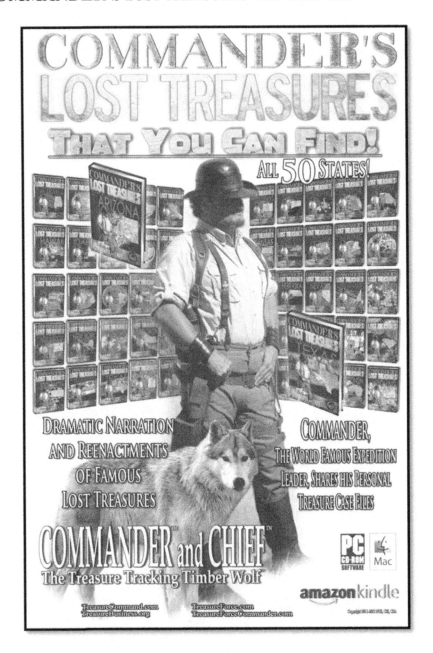

COMMANDER'S
LOST TREASURES

DIGITAL & PRINT ON DEMAND HISTORY BOOKS

LTYCN-ABv1eb
978-1-61973-000-7

978-1-61973-090-8
LTYCN-ABv1pod

LTYCN-AKv1eb
978-1-61973-001-4

978-1-61973-092-2
LTYCN-AKv1pod

LTYCN-AZv1eb
978-1-61973-002-1

978-1-61973-091-5
LTYCN-AZv1pod

LTYCN-ARv1eb
978-1-61973-003-8

978-1-61973-093-9
LTYCN-ARv1pod

LTYCN-CAv1eb
978-1-61973-004-5

978-1-61973-094-6
LTYCN-CAv1pod

LTYCN-COv1eb
978-1-61973-005-2

978-1-61973-095-3
LTYCN-COv1pod

WWW.AMAZON.COM/COMMANDER-PULITZER/E/B00DDWBO52

COMMANDER'S LOST TREASURES

DIGITAL & PRINT ON DEMAND HISTORY BOOKS

LTYCN-CTv1eb
978-1-61973-006-9

978-1-61973-096-0
LTYCN-CTv1pod

LTYCN-DEv1eb
978-1-61973-007-6

978-1-61973-097-7
LTYCN-DEv1pod

LTYCN-FLv1eb
978-1-61973-008-3

978-1-61973-098-4
LTYCN-FLv1pod

LTYCN-GAv1eb
978-1-61973-009-0

978-1-61973-098-4
LTYCN-GAv1pod

LTYCN-HIv1eb
978-1-61973-010-6

978-1-61973-099-1
LTYCN-HIv1pod

LTYCN-IDv1eb
978-1-61973-011-3

978-1-61973-101-1
LTYCN-IDv1pod

WWW.AMAZON.COM/COMMANDER-PULITZER/E/B00DDWBO52

COMMANDER'S
LOST TREASURES

DIGITAL & PRINT ON DEMAND HISTORY BOOKS

LTYCN-ILv1eb
978-1-61973-012-0

978-1-61973-102-8
LTYCN-ILv1pod

LTYCN-INv1eb
978-1-61973-013-7

978-1-61973-103-5
LTYCN-INv1pod

LTYCN-IAv1eb
978-1-61973-014-4

978-1-61973-104-2
LTYCN-IAv1pod

LTYCN-KSv1eb
978-1-61973-015-1

978-1-61973-105-9
LTYCN-KSv1pod

LTYCN-KYv1eb
978-1-61973-016-8

978-1-61973-106-6
LTYCN-KYv1pod

LTYCN-LAv1eb
978-1-61973-017-5

978-1-61973-107-3
LTYCN-LAv1pod

WWW.AMAZON.COM/COMMANDER-PULITZER/E/B00DDWBO52

COMMANDER'S
LOST TREASURES

DIGITAL & PRINT ON DEMAND HISTORY BOOKS

LTYCN-MEv1eb
978-1-61973-018-2

978-1-61973-108-0
LTYCN-MEv1pod

LTYCE-MDv1eb
978-1-61973-019-9

978-1-61973-109-7
LTYCN-MDv1pod

LTYCN-MAv1eb
978-1-61973-020-5

978-1-61973-110-3
LTYCN-MAv1pod

LTYCN-MIv1eb
978-1-61973-021-2

978-1-61973-111-0
LTYCN-MIv1pod

LTYCN-MNv1eb
978-1-61973-022-9

978-1-61973-112-7
LTYCN-MNv1pod

LTYCN-MSv1eb
978-1-61973-023-6

978-1-61973-113-4
LTYCN-MSv1pod

WWW.AMAZON.COM/COMMANDER-PULITZER/E/B00DDWBO52

COMMANDER'S
LOST TREASURES

DIGITAL & PRINT ON DEMAND HISTORY BOOKS

LTYCN-MOv1eb
978-1-61973-024-3

978-1-61973-114-1
LTYCN-MOv1pod

LTYCE-MTv1eb
978-1-61973-025-0

978-1-61973-116-5
LTYCN-MTv1pod

LTYCN-NEv1eb
978-1-61973-026-7

978-1-61973-117-2
LTYCN-NEv1pod

LTYCN-NVv1eb
978-1-61973-027-4

978-1-61973-118-9
LTYCN-NVv1pod

LTYCN-NHv1eb
978-1-61973-028-1

978-1-61973-119-6
LTYCN-NHv1pod

LTYCN-NJv1eb
978-1-61973-029-8

978-1-61973-120-2
LTYCN-NJv1pod

WWW.AMAZON.COM/COMMANDER-PULITZER/E/B00DDWBO52

COMMANDER'S LOST TREASURES YOU CAN FIND

COMMANDER'S
LOST TREASURES
DIGITAL & PRINT ON DEMAND HISTORY BOOKS

LTYCN-NMv1eb
978-1-61973-024-3

978-1-61973-121-9
LTYCN-NMv1pod

LTYCE-NYv1eb
978-1-61973-198-1

978-1-61973-122-6
LTYCN-NYv1pod

LTYCN-NCv1eb
978-1-61973-189-9

978-1-61973-123-3
LTYCN-NCv1pod

LTYCN-NDv1eb
978-1-61973-190-5

978-1-61973-124-0
LTYCN-NDv1pod

LTYCN-OHv1eb
978-1-61973-191-2

978-1-61973-125-7
LTYCN-OHv1pod

LTYCN-OKv1eb
978-1-61973-195-0

978-1-61973-126-4
LTYCN-OKv1pod

WWW.AMAZON.COM/COMMANDER-PULITZER/E/B00DDWBO52

CHAPTER 13 More "Commander" Treasure Books

COMMANDER'S LOST TREASURES

DIGITAL & PRINT ON DEMAND HISTORY BOOKS

LTYCN-ORv1eb
978-1-61973-196-7

978-1-61973-127-1
LTYCN-ORv1pod

LTYCE-PAv1eb
978-1-61973-025-0

978-1-61973-128-8
LTYCN-PAv1pod

LTYCN-RIv1eb
978-1-61973-201-8

978-1-61973-129-5
LTYCN-RIv1pod

LTYCN-SCv1eb
978-1-61973-205-6

978-1-61973-130-1
LTYCN-SCv1pod

LTYCN-SDv1eb
978-1-61973-030-4

978-1-61973-131-8
LTYCN-SDv1pod

LTYCN-TNv1eb
978-1-61973-031-1

978-1-61973-132-5
LTYCN-TNv1pod

WWW.AMAZON.COM/COMMANDER-PULITZER/E/B00DDWBO52

212

COMMANDER'S
LOST TREASURES

DIGITAL & PRINT ON DEMAND HISTORY BOOKS

LTYCN-WIv1eb
978-1-61973-038-0

978-1-61973-140-0
LTYCN-WIv1pod

LTYCE-WYv1eb
978-1-61973-039-7

978-1-61973-139-4
LTYCN-WYv1pod

WWW.AMAZON.COM/COMMANDER-PULITZER/E/B00DDWBO52

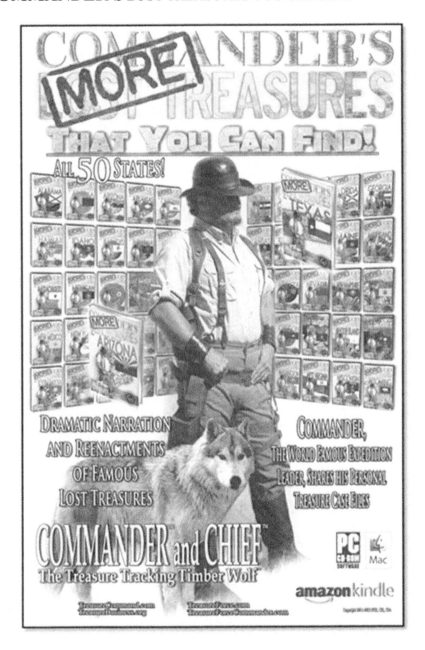

COMMANDER'S MORE LOST TREASURES

DIGITAL & PRINT ON DEMAND HISTORY BOOKS

MLTYCN-ABv2eb
978-1-61973-040-3

978-1-61973-142-4
MLTYCN-ABv2pod

MLTYCN-AKv2eb
978-1-61973-041-0

978-1-61973-141-7
MLTYCN-AKv2pod

MLTYCN-AZv2eb
978-1-61973-042-7

978-1-61973-143-1
MLTYCN-AZv2pod

MLTYCN-ARv2eb
978-1-61973-043-4

978-1-61973-144-8
MLTYCN-ARv2pod

MLTYCN-CAv2eb
978-1-61973-044-1

978-1-61973-146-2
M LTYCN-CAv2pod

MLTYCN-COv2eb
978-1-61973-045-8

978-1-61973-147-9
MLTYCN-COv2pod

WWW.AMAZON.COM/COMMANDER-PULITZER/E/B00DDWBO52

215

DIGITAL & PRINT ON DEMAND HISTORY BOOKS

M LTYCN-CTv2eb
978-1-61973-046-5

978-1-61973-148-6
M LTYCN-CTv2pod

M LTYCN-DEv2eb
978-1-61973-047-2

978-1-61973-149-3
MLTYCN-DEv2pod

MLTYCN-FLv2eb
978-1-61973-048-9

978-1-61973-145-5
MLTYCN-FLv2pod

M LTYCN-GAv2eb
978-1-61973-049-6

978-1-61973-203-2
MLTYCN-GAv2pod

MLTYCN-HIv2eb
978-1-61973-050-2

978-1-61973-150-9
MLTYCN-HIv2pod

MLTYCN-IDv2eb
978-1-61973-051-9

978-1-61973-151-6
MLTYCN-IDv2pod

216

CHAPTER 13 More "Commander" Treasure Books

DIGITAL & PRINT ON DEMAND HISTORY BOOKS

MLTYCN-ILv2eb
978-1-61973-052-6

978-1-61973-152-3
MLTYCN-ILv2pod

MLTYCN-INv2eb
978-1-61973-053-3

978-1-61973-153-0
MLTYCN-INv2pod

MLTYCN-IAv2eb
978-1-61973-054-0

978-1-61973-154-7
MLTYCN-IAv2pod

LTYCN-KSv1eb
978-1-61973-055-7

978-1-61973-155-4
LTYCN-KSv1pod

LTYCN-KYv1eb
978-1-61973-056-4

978-1-61973-156-1
LTYCN-KYv1pod

LTYCN-LAv1eb
978-1-61973-057-1

978-1-61973-157-8
LTYCN-LAv1pod

WWW.AMAZON.COM/COMMANDER-PULITZER/E/B00DDWBO52

217

DIGITAL & PRINT ON DEMAND HISTORY BOOKS

MLTYCN-MEv2eb
978-1-61973-058-8

978-1-61973-158-5
MLTYCN-MEv2pod

MLTYCE-MDv2eb
978-1-61973-059-5

978-1-61973-159-2
MLTYCN-MDv2pod

MLTYCN-MAv2eb
978-1-61973-060-1

978-1-61973-160-8
MLTYCN-MAv2pod

MLTYCN-MIv2eb
978-1-61973-061-8

978-1-61973-161-5
MLTYCN-MIv2pod

MLTYCN-MNv2eb
978-1-61973-062-5

978-1-61973-162-2
MLTYCN-MNv2pod

M LTYCN-MSv2eb
978-1-61973-063-2

978-1-61973-163-9
MLTYCN-MSv2pod

WWW.AMAZON.COM/COMMANDER-PULITZER/E/B00DDWBO52

COMMANDER'S MORE LOST TREASURES

DIGITAL & PRINT ON DEMAND HISTORY BOOKS

MLTYCN-MOv2eb
978-1-61973-064-9

978-1-61973-166-0
MLTYCN-MOv2pod

MLTYCE-MTv2eb
978-1-61973-065-6

978-1-61973-167-7
MLTYCN-MTv2pod

MLTYCN-NEv2eb
978-1-61973-066-3

978-1-61973-168-4
MLTYCN-NEv2pod

MLTYCN-NVv2eb
978-1-61973-067-0

978-1-61973-169-1
MLTYCN-NVv2pod

MLTYCN-NHv2eb
978-1-61973-068-7

978-1-61973-170-7
MLTYCN-NHv2pod

MLTYCN-NJv2eb
978-1-61973-069-4

978-1-61973-171-4
MLTYCN-NJv2pod

WWW.AMAZON.COM/COMMANDER-PULITZER/E/B00DDWBO52

219

DIGITAL & PRINT ON DEMAND HISTORY BOOKS

MLTYCN-NMv2eb
978-1-61973-070-0

978-1-61973-173-8
MLTYCN-NMv2pod

MLTYCE-NYv2eb
978-1-61973-071-7

978-1-61973-163-9
MLTYCN-NYv2pod

MLTYCN-NDv2eb
978-1-61973-072-4

978-1-61973-172-1
MLTYCN-NDv2pod

MLTYCN-NCv2eb
978-1-61973-073-1

978-1-61973-175-2
MLTYCN-NCv2pod

MLTYCN-OHv2eb
978-1-61973-074-8

978-1-61973-199-8
MLTYCN-OHv2pod

MLTYCN-OKv2eb
978-1-61973-075-5

978-1-61973-202-5
MLTYCN-OKv2pod

WWW.AMAZON.COM/COMMANDER-PULITZER/E/B00DDWBO52

220

COMMANDER'S MORE LOST TREASURES

DIGITAL & PRINT ON DEMAND HISTORY BOOKS

MLTYCN-ORv2eb
978-1-61973-076-2

978-1-61973-174-5
MLTYCN-ORv2pod

MLTYCE-PAv2eb
978-1-61973-077-9

978-1-61973-176-9
MLTYCN-PAv2pod

MLTYCN-RIv2eb
978-1-61973-078-6

978-1-61973-177-6
MLTYCN-RIv2pod

MLTYCN-SCv2eb
978-1-61973-079-3

978-1-61973-179-0
MLTYCN-SCv2pod

MLTYCN-SDv2eb
978-1-61973-080-9

978-1-61973-180-6
MLTYCN-SDv2pod

MLTYCN-TNv2eb
978-1-61973-081-6

978-1-61973-181-3
M LTYCN-TNv2pod

WWW.AMAZON.COM/COMMANDER-PULITZER/E/B00DDWBO52

DIGITAL & PRINT ON DEMAND HISTORY BOOKS

MLTYCN-TXv2eb
978-1-61973-082-3

978-1-61973-182-0
MLTYCN-TXv2pod

MLTYCE-UTv2eb
978-1-61973-083-0

978-1-61973-183-7
MLTYCN-UTv2pod

MLTYCN-VTv2eb
978-1-61973-084-7

978-1-61973-184-4
MLTYCN-VTv2pod

MLTYCN-VAv2eb
978-1-61973-085-4

978-1-61973-185-1
MLTYCN-VAv2pod

MLTYCN-WAv2eb
978-1-61973-086-1

978-1-61973-186-8
MLTYCN-WAv2pod

MLTYCN-WIv2eb
978-1-61973-087-8

978-1-61973-187-5
MLTYCN-WIv2pod

WWW.AMAZON.COM/COMMANDER-PULITZER/E/B00DDWBO52

222

DIGITAL & PRINT ON DEMAND HISTORY BOOKS

M LTYCN-Wlv2eb
978-1-61973-088-5

MLTYCE-WYv2eb
978-1-61973-089-2

978-1-61973-192-9
M LTYCN-Wlv2pod

978-1-61973-193-6
MLTYCN-WYv2pod

WWW.AMAZON.COM/COMMANDER-PULITZER/E/B00DDWBO52

CHAPTER 14

Become a Certified Cacheologist

Become a Certified Cacheologist

In a world with literally Billions upon Billions of unrecovered Treasures and Riches, more individuals are turning to the world of Cacheology and seeking their Professional Accreditation as a Certified Cacheologist. Around the globe, more and more multi-million dollar treasures are being recovered by these individuals that all the University and Government Branches combined. Now you can take your passion for History, Collecting, Adventure and Treasure Hunting and turn it into a Profitable Career. Why is this opportunity now possible?

At the University and Government level, funding for professional cache exploration and recovery is literally zero. The current tide of funds within University and Government institutions are directed by the current political and "what's politically correct" environment and the focus is on the obfuscation of history and its treasure rather than the discovery of true and accurate history and the sharing of that history and treasure with the world, unedited and without political motivation. Thus the Professional Cacheologist is now a professional in high demand by a society that wants the truth of its collective history and not the "sanitized approved version" The world, with the advent of the Internet and social networking now want their information raw, directly from the original source and not reworked by editors. Nowadays, this "direct to the public approach", unedited, transparent and available to all is not only the new standard, but the battle cry of an enlightened individual.

Can you imagine yourself as a real life Indiana Jones? Could you imagine yourself as going down in history as the person who found that long lost city or civilization or the individual that found the keys to decoding long lost languages that prove the history of the world as we have been taught **IS WRONG**? This could be you as a Professional Cacheologist!

When it comes to history and cache recovery, Cacheologists are leading the way in this Movement of Pure Truth and are recovering the worlds **REAL HISTROY** and making it available to the World directly. Not to mention, Cacheologists are becoming both Millionaires and Billionaires in the process of leading this charge for the Truth and Recovery.

Do you want an exciting new career that will eventually be credited with rewriting the history of the world as we know it? Do you want to be on the leading edge of recovering the lost billions and billions in treasure and history that has been lost to the world? Are you ready for a career unlike any other career known to man?

What is Cacheology?

In the world of Treasure Hunting or more appropriately Cache Exploration and Recovery there are those who are enthusiasts or recreational minded individuals with the opposite end of the spectrum being the Professional Cache Recovery Expert; know as a Cacheologists in the field of Cacheology.

CACHEOLOGY: The profession, whereby highly trained and certified individuals, using archaeological methods combined with forensic historical re- search and modern technology, set out to either prove or disprove, dispel or recover, set the historical record straight or professional document, the various types of caches, common treasures or otherwise, that have been lost to history and mankind. The mission of the Cacheologist is to recover lost caches, for the expansion of mankind's study, education, instruction, collecting, showcasing, and preservation. The professional rescue and preservation of caches that time and the environment rapidly and thoroughly destroy, thus erasing vital and irreplaceable historical records and artifacts of the entire world.

CHAPTER 14 Become a Certified Cacheologist

GEOCACHEOLOGIST: A specialized discipline and field of study within Cacheology, dealing specifically with the use of archaeological methods combined with forensic historical research, geochemical prospecting, field exploration and modern technology, set out to either; prove or disprove, dispel and/or set the historical record straight and professionally document the myths, legends and/or accounts of lost mines and/or geological caches.

MYTHOCHRONOLOGIST: A specialized discipline and field of study within Cacheology, dealing specifically with the use of archaeological methods, advanced research methods, forensic historical research and modern technology, set out to either; prove or disprove, dispel and/or set the historical record straight and professionally document the dates of, participants in, location of and the historical retelling of various myths, legends and/or accounts of lost caches. A Mythochronologist may participate in field exploration for the recreation of the events of a particular myth, legend or account of a lost cache for the specific purpose of scientifically verifying the details, events and circum- stances of lost caches.

CACHEOLOGICAL HISTORIAN: A specialized discipline and field of study within Cacheology, dealing specifically with the use of archaeological methods, advanced research methods, forensic historical research and modern technology, set out to either; prove or disprove, dispel and/or set the historical record straight and professionally document the dates of, participants in, location of and the historical retelling of various myths, legends and/or accounts of lost caches **SPECIFICALLY** for the purpose of publication of the details, events and circumstances of lost caches. A Cacheological Historian may participate in field to be able to recount and document events, circumstances from an immersion in the actual historical location from a first person perspective.

_•_

Those who are enthusiasts or recreational treasure hunters pursue treasure hunting, metal detecting or rock hounding to occupy their spare or vacation time and create fun and exciting memories. But many times these enthusiasts or recreational minded individuals find themselves in massive legal entanglements which come with huge legal fees and possible imprisonment, just for accidentally finding a Lost Treasure and making it known.

What good would it do such individuals to accidentally find a million dollar treasure or artifact to only have their find yanked from them by authorities and themselves heavily fined? But becoming a Certified Cacheologist assures you (a) know what you are doing, (b) do it within the legal boundaries and laws, (c) are able to profit from your activities and profit **BIG**!

CHAPTER 14 Become a Certified Cacheologist

This is where becoming a professional Cacheologist is rapidly becoming the chosen certification and profession for those individuals who have that adventurous spirit and nature that calls them to recovery lost history and its treasures. Did you even know there was such a certification and profession? You surely have of heard of the profession of Archaeologist, but what about the Archaeology minded individual who specifically focuses on the lost treasures of the recent and ancient past? This is a Cacheologist. In fact, the popular action hero Indiana Jones, is in fact a **CACHEOLOGIST** rather than an Archaeologist, but now Cacheologist and Archaeologists can go hand in hand and uncover the past and discover the Pure Truth.

_-•-_

Below is the Professional Description and Classification of a Certified Cacheologist, as provided by the Cacheology Society and Institute of the UK (the foreign governing body for Cacheologists) and the Cacheology Society of America (the domestic governing and certification body in the United States for Cacheologist):

Cacheology:

"Archaeological methods combined with forensic historical research and the profession, whereby highly trained and certified individuals, using modern technology, set out to either prove or disprove, dispel or recover, set the historical record straight or professionally document, the various types of caches, common treasures or otherwise, that have been lost to history and mankind. The mission of the Cacheologists is to recover lost caches, using profit driven methods, for the expansion of mankind's study, education, instruction, collecting, showcasing, and preservation. The professional rescue and preservation of caches that time and the environment rapidly and thoroughly destroy, thus erasing vital and irreplaceable historical records and artifacts of the entire world."

Currently the world is faced with an ever increasing dilemma, "Archaeology, its administration, governance and accreditation is controlled by politically minded Institutions with little or no exploration and recovery funding and even less motivational capital to bring to the public new and exciting discoveries that reveal the true and accurate account of history. Therefore, history changing discoveries are suppressed and warehoused so not to conflict with benefactors, political agendas and the current prevailing politically corrected line of thought".

It is easy to see the dilemma here. Lost Treasures, Lost Societies and Lost History belong to the world as whole. Thus, the exploration, discovery and recovery of these things must be open to the collective of the world and not obscured, hidden, hoarded by any institutional system, but must be equally made available to the field of studies, public display and public and private collections and ownership.

This is where your **NEW CAREER** as a Professional Cacheologist comes in. The exciting and adventurous field of Cacheology is the bridge between Institutions and the Public's quest for the Truth, the Pure Truth. You, as a Professional Cacheologist **CAN** go hunt for those Lost Treasure and Lost History on your own! You don't have to play political games, get approval from a stuffy Board of Directors or even get approval from your Boss to go after a Lost Treasure or stash of Gold. Why? **YOU ARE YOUR OWN BOSS**. As a Professional Cacheologist, you make your schedule; you make your agenda and expedition schedule. Adventure is waiting.

AS A CERTIFIED PROFESSIONAL CACHEOLOGIST YOU NOT ONLY HUNT FOR LOST TREASURES, LOST CITIES,

LOST HISTORY AND HIGHLY VALUABLE ARTIFACTS, BUT YOU COULD:

1. Be called upon by a Local, State or Federal Government to recover these items

2. Be called upon by a Foreign Government to recover these items,

3. Be called upon by Private Investors or even Institutions to put together an Expedition to find and recover such items, and;

4. You could even be called on by a Private Land Owner to find something they lost or a long lost family Cache on private family land.

The opportunities are endless.

When you choose to become a Certified Personal Cacheologist, there are three levels of Certification and Private Accreditation. They are:

1. Certified Cacheologist, CC, CSA
2. Certified Cacheologist, CC, CSI
3. Certified Cacheologist, CC, CSI, ACE

Imagine these Prestigious Certification Credentials on your personal business cards, stationary, books, videos, News Interviews, and published articles about your efforts and adventures!

LET'S TAKE A CLOSER LOOK AT EACH SET OF PROFESSIONAL CREDENTIALS AND WHAT THEY STAND FOR.

• **CERTIFIED CACHEOLOGIST, CC, CSA**

COMMANDER'S LOST TREASURES YOU CAN FIND

A Certified Cacheologist with the designation of CC, CSA means they have been certified by the Cacheology Society of America and have completed a rigorous course of study (see below) in Cacheology and have completed the required Course Work and Certification of the Cacheology Society of America and are a member in good standing. It's not too dissimilar from the training of a Real Estate Agent and the required certification to become a Realtor. CC, stands for Certified Cacheologist and CSA, stand for the Agency of Accreditation and Certification, the Cacheology Society of America. At this level of Certification and Accreditation you are certified in the Treasure and Recovery Laws of the United States of America, on both a national and State by State level.

• CERTIFIED CACHEOLOGIST, CC, CSI

A Certified Cacheologist with the designation of CC, CSI means they have been certified by the Cacheology Society and Institute, UK and can operate on both a US and International Level. You have completed a rigorous course of study (see below) in Cacheology and have completed the required Course Work and Certification of the Cacheology Society and Institute, UK and are a member in good standing. It's not too dissimilar from the training of a Real Estate Agent and the required certification to become a Realtor, in the US. CC, stands for Certified Cacheologist and CSI, stand for the Agency of Accreditation and Certification, the Cacheology Society and Institute, UK and you are also of the same standing within the Cacheology Society of America. One cannot move up to the CSI Accreditation without achieving the CSA Accreditation initially. At this level of Certification and Accreditation you are certified in the Treasure and Recovery Laws of the United States of America, on both a national and State by State level AND you are certified in the Treasure and Recovery Laws of the European, Latin and other Major Nations, on both a Region and County by Country level.

• CERTIFIED CACHEOLOGIST, CC, CSI OR CSA, ACE

A Certified Cacheologist with the FINAL DESIGNATION AND ACCREDITA- TION of ACE is the pinnacle of Cacheology Certification. The ACE level can be achieved by both the CSA and CSI certifications. The ACE means you have not only achieved your Certification as a Cacheologist, but you have attended the Multi-Thousand Acre Outdoor Campus and Training Facility of the Cacheology Society and Institute, UK and Cacheology Society of America. You get to manage and conduct LIVE Expeditions in real time with the latest and most advanced Technology available to Cacheologists (see: Cacheology University and it's one of a kind campus below). Within this Multi-Thousand Acre Training Facility you will find, decode and follow real clues and signs to real treasures and be placed in situations that require you to master, mountains, hills, woods, forests, streams, deep water recovery, island recovery and even underground recovery.

The Cacheology Society and Institute and Cacheology Society of America have put together the most extensive syllabus for the comprehensive training and certification on prospective Cacheologists of any learning institution.

Here is a partial sample of what a Cacheologist' education

CHAPTER 14 Become a Certified Cacheologist

looks like:

www.ExpeditionHistory.org   Copy 2014 JHP   www.TREASUREFORCE.com

Top 25 Unrecovered Caches by State

Caches – Alabama

Caches – Alaska

Caches– Arizona

Caches – Arkansas

Caches – California

Caches – Colorado

Caches – Connecticut

Caches – Delaware

Caches – Florida

Caches – Georgia

Caches – Hawaii

Caches – Idaho

Caches – Illinois

Caches – Indiana

Caches – Iowa

Caches – Kansas

Caches – Kentucky

Caches – Louisiana

Caches – Maine

Caches – Maryland

Caches – Massachusetts

Caches – Michigan

Caches – Minnesota

Caches – Mississippi

Caches – Missouri

Caches – Montana

Caches – Nebraska

Caches – Nevada

Caches – New Hampshire

Caches – New Jersey

Caches – New Mexico

Caches – New York

Caches – North Carolina

Caches – North Dakota

Caches – Ohio

Caches – Oklahoma

Caches – Oregon

Caches – Pennsylvania

Caches – Rhode Island

Caches – South Carolina

Caches – South Dakota

Caches – Tennessee

Caches – Texas

Caches – Utah

Caches – Vermont

Caches – Virginia

Caches – Washington

Caches – West Virginia

Caches – Wisconsin

Caches – Wyoming

Underwater Caches
and Historical Research

Terrestrial Caches
and Historical Research

Researching Historical Periodicals and News Sources

Now that you have read over the extensive education a Cacheologist receives it is easy to see why the Cacheology Society and Institute and Cacheology Society of America have put together the most extensive syllabus for the comprehensive training and certification on prospective Cacheologist of any learning institution in the world.

Your training and certification covers every single aspect a Professional Cacheologist need to be proficient in to really be successful in this multi-billion dollar opportunity for discovery and recovery.

Now let's go to Cacheology University. Mountains, Rivers, Caves, Rocks, Boulders, Deep Water Spring Fed Lake over 100 Miles of Shoreline with over 20 Islands and Thousands of Acres!

Now imagine the wonderful Cacheology education you receive and then getting real time, hands on training by a Professional Cacheologist. That is what the **ACE** certification is – the final professional step in your Advanced Training. As you read, a Certified Cacheologist with the **FINAL DESIGNATION AND ACCREDITATION** of **ACE** is the pinnacle of Cacheology Certification. The **ACE** level can be achieved by both the **CSA** and **CSI** certifications. The **ACE** means you have not only achieved your Certification as a Cacheologist, but you have attended and graduated the Cacheology Outdoor University.

COMMANDER'S LOST TREASURES YOU CAN FIND

The Cacheology University is the Multi-Thousand Acre Outdoor Campus and Training Facility of the Cacheology Society and Institute, UK and Cacheology Society of America. Here you get the opportunity to manage and conduct a **LIVE** Expedition in real time with the latest and most advanced Technology available to Cacheologists. Within this Multi-Thousand Acre Training Facility you will find, decode and follow real clues and signs to real treasures and be placed in situations that require you to master mountains, hills, woods, forests, streams, deep water recovery, island recovery and even underground recovery.

CHAPTER 14 Become a Certified Cacheologist

At Cacheology University you will find almost every single type or potential Cache environment. You and your other attendees will conduct a three pronged Cache Expedition, practicing each and every aspect of your Cacheology Certification and Training. Mountains, Rivers, Caves, Rocks, Boulders, Deep Water Spring Fed Lake over 100 Miles of Shoreline with over 20 Islands and Thousands of Acres!

Imagine following Ancient Spanish Treasure Symbols to find the Lost Treasure. Imagine not recognizing a Spanish death trap and your expedition is set back. Follow clues, investigate ruins, read the terrain, scale mountains, execute rescue and extraction maneuvers, use the latest Cacheology Technology including.

- Ground Penetrating Radar
- Forensic Cache Research and Documentation
- Advanced Metal Detecting
- Ultra-light Reconnaissance
- Base Camp Management
- Expedition Medical Safety
- Photo Reconnaissance
- Wilderness Survival
- 4x4 and Extreme Transportation
- Mountain Climbing and Rappelling
- Cave Exploration
- Deep Water Reconnaissance
- Underwater Remote Operated Vehicles
- (R. O. V. s)
- Aerial Reconnaissance
- with Unmanned Aerial Vehicles
- (U. A. V. s)
- Cache Site and Mineral Forensics
- GPS Mapping and Navigation

These are a few of the programs and things you will be doing to gain your A. C. E. advanced Cacheologist Certification while at your one week stay at Cacheology University in the midst of Mountains, Rivers, Caves, Rocks, Boulders, Deep Water Spring Fed Lake over 100 Miles of Shoreline with over 20 Islands and Thousands of Acres!

The C. S. A. and C. S. I. Certifications is self paced and an online study program. More information on tuition and enrollment can be found at:

TODAY COULD BE THE DAY YOU DECIDE TO

CHANGE YOUR LIFE

AND ENTER THE WORLD'S MOST EXCITING PROFESSION AND BECOME A CERTIFIED CACHEOLOGIST!

Made in the USA
Coppell, TX
04 November 2020

40782633R00138